Active Assemblies for Every Week

Jenny Mosley and Ross Grogan

**36 assemblies for each week of the school year
grouped into themes for teaching the
Social and Emotional Aspects of Learning**

Published in 2006 by:
Positive Press Ltd
28A Gloucester Road
Trowbridge
Wiltshire BA14 0AA

Telephone: 01225 719204
Fax: 01225 712187
E-mail: positivepress@jennymosley.co.uk
Website: www.circle-time.co.uk

Text © Jenny Mosley and Ross Grogan
Reprinted 2007, 2009
ISBN **978 190 4866 190**

Photography by Viewpoint, Somerset

Printed by:
Heron Press
White Hays North
West Wilts Trading Estate
Westbury
Wiltshire BA13 4JT

Contents

How to use this book   3

RE and the curriculum   4

Getting ready   4

How to present an assembly   5

Six steps to a successful assembly   8

NEW BEGINNINGS   11

Welcome!   12
Put everyone at ease as part of a
shared community.

Pocahontas   14
Explore how we get to know each
other and make friends.

The gingerbread man   16
Develop a sense of the whole-school
community.

Bundle of sticks   18
Investigate the advantages of a
cohesive group.

Two and two can make five!   20
We can share all our skills and talents
for the benefit of everyone.

Taking care   22
We need to look after the equipment
we use so that everyone can share the
things they need to work and play
happily.

Get sorted   25
Don't waste your time, or other
people's time. It is precious!

GETTING ON AND FALLING OUT   29

What's on the menu?   30
Investigate the qualities we look for in
our friends.

The way I see it   32
Encourage respect for differing points
of view.

The caucus race   34
Understand the difference between
fact and opinion and see how this
knowledge has a positive effect on
social interaction.

Rough with the smooth   37
When things go wrong we can look for
the positive to make matters better.

Break friends, make friends   40
Investigate the power of forgiveness.

A few of my useful things   43
Consider the function of rules and why
it is important that rules are kept.

SAY NO TO BULLYING   47

Fairy godmothers   48
Telling a grown-up about bullying is
a way of helping others.

You don't scare me, Mr Lion   50
Look at strategies for facing our fears.

What would you do?   53
Address peer-group pressure by
developing refusal skills and ways of
saying 'no'.

CONTENTS

GOING FOR GOALS   **57**

One step at a time   **58**
We need to have the patience to learn things step by step if we are to reach our goals.

Treasure seekers   **60**
We can set and achieve our goals.

The best possible plan   **62**
Problems can be solved by taking positive steps.

Look before you leap   **66**
Consider the consequences of our actions.

GOOD TO BE ME   **69**

Seed of a smile   **70**
We can scatter the seeds of self-belief and success.

Sunny side up   **72**
Look at moods and how we can make ourselves happier from day to day.

Each and every one of us   **74**
Every one of us is a very special person.

The variety of life   **76**
Celebrate diversity and be proud of who we are.

In the town of Trigatree   **78**
Develop awareness of cultural diversity.

For the reason that follows   **80**
Demonstrate the importance of being able to justify an opinion.

The air that we breathe   **82**
Fitness and health makes us feel good.

RELATIONSHIPS   **85**

What can I do for you?   **86**
Investigate what it means to be unselfish.

Easy life   **89**
Look at the ways we can help teachers and support staff in school.

Keeping steady   **91**
Investigate strategies that help us to balance our moods.

The frog prince   **93**
Consider what it means to keep a promise.

Watch me use my ears   **96**
Develop the skill of attentive listening.

Helping Henry   **98**
Appreciate the people who care for us.

Twinkle   **100**
Illustrate the importance of caring for each other.

CHANGES   **103**

Time for a change   **104**
Investigate the process of change.

Butterfly school   **107**
Celebrate children's achievements over the year.

How to use this book

The *Active Assemblies for Every Week* collection is arranged in themes that reflect the guidance materials for Social and Emotional Aspects of Learning (SEAL) from the Primary National Strategy. These include: new beginnings, getting on and falling out, say no to bullying, going for goals, good to be me, relationships, and changes. There is only one example assembly in the SEAL guidance. Active Assemblies provides a rich resource of different approaches to each theme, to provide inspiring assemblies which reinforce the ethos of happy, effective schools.

Every school is a community in which individuals study and play together as members of an interdependent group whose purpose is to achieve common goals. Successful schools recognise that solidarity is impossible without shared values and moral beliefs and they build a strong sense of community by paying active attention to the kinds of social order and cooperation that they wish to encourage and promote. High quality assemblies enable everybody in the community to come together to learn about and understand the values and ambitions that underpin your school ethos and to prepare children to live as successful members of our wider society.

Assemblies have a special rhythm of their own that sets them apart from ordinary lessons. The combination of drama and reverence, interaction and solitary reflection makes a daily ritual that is a vital and life enhancing part of each and every school day. They offer children an opportunity to reflect upon their rights and responsibilities as members of a social group that is so much more than a sum of its parts. During assembly, adults are able to communicate the school's vision and to model the values and skills that they wish children to emulate. Younger children learn about the roles they will play as they progress through the school because they are shown the way by older pupils.

This book will show you how to deliver meaningful assemblies that will engage your pupils and get them thinking. The 36 assemblies are designed to teach a range of universal values and skills that will help you to create a culture of success and harmony by teaching sensitivity to the needs of others alongside self-awareness. Children can learn how to behave as members of a purposeful community. You will be able to deliver assemblies with confidence and charisma, capture attention and model thinking skills and reflection in ways that are accessible to a wide range of children. You can relate your school values to children's real, lived, experience by planning assemblies that are uniquely suited to your particular school.

The assemblies in this book follow a three-step structure: opening, development and reflection. Each stage is explained and model scripts, in italics, are offered to deliver the key points which can be adapted as you wish.

RE and the curriculum

The Education Act (1944) requires that Collective Worship should be 'wholly or mainly of a broadly Christian character' but that the precise nature will depend on 'the family background, ages and abilities of pupils'. Each assembly in this book is designed to teach social and emotional aspects of learning (SEAL) and are arranged to fit in with QCA guidelines. They are not, as they stand, acts of Collective Worship. They do, however, reflect moral values and behaviours that are consistent with religious teaching because they stress the importance of caring for one another alongside the experience of quiet contemplation. The opening and reflective phases of each assembly can be adapted to incorporate worship and prayer by small changes in the wording in accordance with your policy for Collective Worship. For example, the reflection can be altered to include thanks to God and requests for his help in achieving a harmonious world and can then be used as prayers.

Getting Ready

Excellent assemblies require thorough preparation. You need to read through each 'script' before you begin and check that it is appropriate for your particular school. Don't be afraid to make changes to suit your needs. Make sure that you have collected all the equipment that will be required and that CD players and electrical equipment are plugged in and ready to use. Most importantly, think carefully about the theme so that it is uppermost in your mind throughout assembly time – this is the point of the meeting and you must never lose sight of it.

Think about the space you will be using:

- Can you reach all of your equipment easily and smoothly?

- Do you need performance space? Will there be sufficient space for the particular performance that you wish to do?

- Will the audience be able to see all of the performance without wriggling and getting frustrated?

- Do you need to create pathways so that the audience can reach the front easily?

- Is your visual focus big enough to be seen/read by children at the back? Do you need to put the flip chart on a platform? Do you need to put your range of objects on to a display table?

- Is there room to vary the seating arrangements sometimes? Can some assemblies take place in the round?

- Do you have a stock of classical music to set the mood as children enter and leave the assembly? Instrumental music immediately quietens children and creates a 'listening' atmosphere that sets assembly apart from other parts of the school day. Music ensures that all the participants are calm and ready to consider the valuable theme you have chosen for each assembly. Almost all classical music has this effect and compilation discs are available in stores if you want to experiment and find just the right music for your children. Music can also be used during the assembly to give space for private thought. Play it quietly at times when you want the children to sit and imagine or consider important issues or when you wish to prepare them for the reflection stage of the assembly.

How to present an assembly

Begin and end in an atmosphere of contemplation

One of the main functions of assembly time is to teach children the importance of reflective thought, so each meeting should begin and end in a friendly but quiet way. It is the leader's responsibility to ensure that this happens by modelling the expected behaviour. Welcome the children quietly by sitting at the front and remaining very still and calm. The time for activity will come but these first moments of quietude are essential if you are to convey the right frame of mind. This is also true of the reflective stage which ends the meeting. Never rush these stages. Wait until everyone is still and tranquil; speak softly and slowly and ensure that the atmosphere of contemplation is maintained as the assembly ends and each class quietly leaves the hall.

Communicate, don't 'talk at' your audience

You have valuable, life-enriching messages to get across so you need to ensure that your audience is instantly involved and attentive. A question or a show of hands is a good way to achieve instant attention. For example, if your theme is the benefits of working as a team, begin the assembly with a show of hands from those who have worked in a team recently. Who enjoyed the experience? Who plays in a sports team? Then begin the opening phase of the assembly. All of the assemblies in this book are interactive but you can always insert more questions and answers as you go along to ensure that you keep the children alert and attentive. A snippet of self-disclosure always intrigues children and you will find that the whole school will pay close attention if you introduce the assembly by saying something personal, such as, 'I went to a meeting after school yesterday and the leader asked me to sit next to a teacher from another school and…' or 'When I was ten we moved to Newcastle and…'. Link this 'disclosure' to your theme and you will be able to slide seamlessly into your assembly with everybody's full attention. Personal stories help the children to link emotionally to the theme of the assembly and help them to realise that you are talking about things that are real and relevant to their own lives.

Be a good listener

Active assemblies are a wonderful opportunity to model pro-social behaviours especially during the interactive phases. You can demonstrate how to be a good listener when you take contributions from the audience. Good listeners tend to be physically still and attentive and make 'I am listening' indications to show that they are interested and know how to feedback to show that they have understood. You also need to ensure that you make appropriate eye contact.

If you don't look at someone when you are talking or listening to him or her they will naturally suppose that you are not truly interested in what they are saying.

Vary your tone of voice

The music you play when the children enter the assembly is captivating because it conveys atmosphere and mood through changes in volume and pace and you need to maintain attention by using the same device – by speaking in a variety of different ways that ensure that no-one drifts off into a little reverie while you speak. Slow down when you are speaking of something dramatic and speed up when you want to convey excitement. Pause sometimes to allow children to think about your message or to create a dramatic effect. Try to help them to understand what you are saying by showing facial expression as you speak and use gesture and body language to explain what you mean. Don't forget to move forward, bend and smile when you ask children about their thoughts and opinions and always thank them for their contributions.

Add a dash of humour

You don't need to be a comedian but a light touch of humour every now and then will make everyone feel comfortable and relaxed. Interludes of humour need to be brief and to the point but they capture attention and mean that the children will view you as a kind, amiable person who has their best interests at heart and wants them to be happy. This, in turn, makes them more accepting and receptive to what you have to say. A witty comment or a funny walk will do the trick nicely: children love to laugh and you will feel energised yourself when you hear the whole school unite in a chuckle or a smile.

Make the most of your helpers

Initially, the prospect of leading an assembly can feel intimidating but remember you don't need to be all alone at the front for long. There are bound to be children in the audience who just love to perform and all you need to do is adapt the assembly so that they are invited up as quickly as possible. You can always prepare a group in advance or teach your class a relevant song and add that to the beginning of the assembly plan.

Don't forget that the props are there to help you

If the prospect of standing at the front makes you self-conscious and tongue-tied, then make sure that you have some interesting props. All the time the audience is captivated by the intriguing artefact or by guessing just what you have hidden in that big sack, they won't be looking at you and you can catch your breath and steady your nerves for a moment. Be reassured by the fact that, as you do more assemblies, your confidence will grow and you will find that you enjoy them more and more.

Planning you own assemblies

When you have used the thirty-six assemblies in this book you will have lots of experience and may wish to design assemblies of your own. The following tips will help you to deliver assemblies that are uniquely suited to your particular school.

Six steps to creating a successful assembly

1. Think of a theme

What is the point you want to make? This is your focus and you need to be very clear about it. Fix it in your planning with a single sentence. It may be a practical issue like 'We don't waste paper' or, alternatively, it may involve a complicated moral issue like bullying. If you need to examine such a complex issue, then you must choose a single, specific aspect of the issue and concentrate on that.

2. Keep it simple

This is probably the most important 'golden rule'. When you have your idea, try to plan your assembly so that you are focussing on one part of the subject at a time. Otherwise children will become confused and learn very little.

3. Ensure understanding

Check that the children share your understanding of the key words in your theme. It is probable that one word will be pivotal in any assembly so it is vital that everyone has a common understanding of what you mean by it. It would, for instance, be futile to hold an assembly about co-operation if some of your children think that you are talking about the local co-op shop! You need to explain, clarify and demonstrate the meaning of your key words throughout the assembly if the value they represent is to be understood and practised by all the children in the school.

4. Illustrate your point

Jesus used parables to explain abstract moral values and you need to do something similar for children by converting your focus into something concrete and visual. You need to show, as well as tell. It can seem difficult to dream up a suitable visual metaphor but it is well worth the effort because it turns your assembly into a memorable dramatic event that is a useful reference point for the children as they struggle to understand complex moral issues.

5. Use familiar props

You are making a point and you are making it in a visual way but you don't want the props to be too distracting. If the children are trying to work out what the props are, they won't be listening to the point that you are making. This is actually to your benefit because it means that you only need to use everyday things. It's the way you utilise objects from home, or school equipment, that will make all the difference.

6. Reinforce the theme

Having shown, clarified and explained your point during the assembly, you need to end by repeating this very clearly. This can often be done as a prayer or moment of reflection. The message that the children take back to class should be the same simple sentence that began your planning.

New beginnings

The beginning of a new school year or term is always exciting. Whether starting school or moving up a year, there are new teachers and children to meet and it's a time to feel good about being part of a shared community. It's all about belonging and looking at ways of making that community work happily for everyone. You can take the fresh start of a new year to reaffirm the ethos of your school, and show everyone that they have a part to play in shaping the character of their classrooms.

This section begins with 'Welcome!' and 'Pocahontas' two reassuring assemblies that focus on putting people at their ease. The next step is to get to know everyone who helps in the school with the aid of 'The gingerbread man'.

A happy school is a school that works together, where everyone is proud to play their part. Aesop's fable 'The bundle of sticks' is used here to emphasise how we can enjoy the support of a strong community. 'Two and two can make five' reminds us that EVERYONE has a unique contribution to make to the recipe for an exciting, successful learning environment.

The theme closes with reminders of the ways children can make life easier for everyone else with some care and consideration. The golden rules of 'look after property' and 'don't waste time' are explored in 'Taking care' and 'Get sorted'.

Welcome!

Focus

To welcome everyone and put them at ease as part of a shared community.

You will need

Seven large pieces of card, each card having one letter – C, E, E, L, M, W, O – an additional piece of card with the letter 'L' written on it; a flipchart.

Opening

Hold up the first card and ask, 'Who has a name that begins with this letter?' Choose a child to come up and hold the card. Continue until all the letter cards are taken. Then look at the line of cards, scratch your head and state that you can't seem to make any sense of the letter string. Rearrange the children to make another nonsense word. Try to sound it out. When you have got the children's attention and have them trying to fathom out the word, you can arrange it into the word WELCOME. Can anyone help to explain why you have made that particular word? Take the opportunity to welcome everyone back to school – say how glad you are to see them all and how much you are looking forward to the new term.

▶ Development

Lead the children through the rest of the assembly using this script:

Welcome is a happy word. When we welcome someone into our home or school it means that we are glad to see him or her. Welcome is made from two words squashed together.
(Move the children into two groups to demonstrate this.)
This first word is 'WELL' but the 'Ls' have got squeezed into one. I will put the other 'L' back in, just for a minute, while they are being two separate words.
(Ask a child to come forward to hold the second 'L'.)
'Well' is a happy word. We use it to say good things, like 'You did that piece of

writing very well' or 'I am feeling very well and healthy today'.
(Now move to the second group of children.)
The second part of the word is 'come' which means 'to move towards someone'. If I say 'Come here, Mr Brown,' you all know what I want Mr Brown to do, don't you?
(Quietly ask the last child to give you back the 'L' and return to their seat. Make the two parts into one word again.)
So now you see that when we say 'welcome' we are saying that we are very pleased to meet someone and that we are happy in his or her company. Welcome is a helpful word too. When someone says 'Can I borrow your felt pen?' we can answer 'You are welcome', which means 'I like you and I trust you, so of course you can'. A welcoming face has a very special look that tells us that someone is glad to see us. I am going to turn my back for a moment and, when I face you again, you have to say 'yes' or 'no', depending on whether my face is welcoming or not welcoming.
(Turn around with a cross face and then again with a welcoming smiling face.)
Which face did you like best? The welcoming face! Classrooms can be welcoming too. We want everyone in this school to feel happy in our classrooms. Who has some ideas about how we can have classrooms where everyone feels welcome and happy?
(Take suggestions from the floor. Write them on your flipchart.)
Well, that is an excellent list of things that we can do to make our classrooms feel really welcome. It's so good that I think I will get it typed up so that everyone can have a copy for their classroom wall.

Reflection

People like to feel welcome. It makes us feel warm and happy and wanted. We can show that we are welcoming with our expression and the way that we move and the way we speak. We can say 'you are welcome' and make other people smile. We can make our rooms welcoming so that people feel relaxed and happy as they come through the door. Let's all welcome each other back to school today and let's make every day a happy 'you're welcome' day.

Pocahontas

 Focus

This assembly explores how we get to know each other and make friends.

 You will need

A flip-chart and pens.

 Opening

Explain to the children that sometimes our friends and family don't call us by our real name but give us a nickname or pet-name instead. Explain how people get nicknames and give some examples: 'Dusty' Miller (from the surname suggesting flour), 'Billy Whizz' (from a skill or characteristic). Be careful to emphasise that these are nicknames given with fondness and only by family and friends.

Development

▶▶ Tell the assembly that today you're going to think about a girl whose real name was Matoaka. She was a Native American princess who lived a long time ago. She loved to dance and be happy so she was given the pet-name 'Pocahontas', which in her language means 'little playful one'. Now tell the story…

A group of Englishmen led by Captain John Smith landed in America near where Pocahontas lived. She had never seen people with such pale skin, dressed in strange sailors' clothes with heavy boots on their feet and sailors' hats on their heads. Pocahontas and her tribe could not speak a single word of English and John Smith and his sailors could speak no Algonquian, which was her language.

Ask for volunteers to show what it must have been like when the characters in the story met. They will need to get to know one another and make friends but they CANNOT use any words – they will have to use other ways of communicating. When the children have watched these mimes, make a list of the things we say when we meet, like 'Hi, how are you?' and 'I'm fine, thanks'. Ask the children in pairs to invent sign language ways of 'saying' these things without words. Ask for volunteers to come forward and demonstrate their sign language and point out the body language they will also be using: leaning forward, smiling and so on.

Reflection

When we meet people that we don't yet know – when new children start at school for example, or when we are on holiday – we have seen that our body language, the way we behave and the effort that we put in can make a big difference to how the other person will feel about us. If we behave in a friendly way they will feel at ease and will want to get to know us better. Let's all think of ways to make everyone a potential new friend.

The gingerbread man

 Focus

To develop a sense of the whole-school community.

 You will need

A copy of the story of the gingerbread man; a cut-out figure of a gingerbread man; a squeaker; as many members of staff as you can muster.

 Opening

Begin by reading the story of the gingerbread man to the assembly. Discuss how, on his journey, he met many different people and animals. Afterwards, ask the children if they can remember who he met and what happened in the story. Now press the squeaker, and use this script:

What's that noise? It's coming from my bag. What could be in there? Let me have a look. Goodness me, it's a gingerbread man. He must have run away from the oven and somehow got stuck in my bag.
(Hold up the cut-out figure of a gingerbread man for everybody to see. Make the squeaking noise again.)
What's that, gingerbread man? Do you want to say something?
(Hold the gingerbread man to your ear and pretend to listen.)
He's telling me that he has come into school today because he wants to meet some of the people who work here. Who would you like to meet, gingerbread man?
(Hold him to your ear again.)
He says that he would like to meet that person over there.
(Choose a member of staff and ask her a few questions – name, job title, where she can be found, and a little bit about her work. In this way, you can 'interview' as many members of staff as you wish. When this process is complete, tell the children that the gingerbread man is very pleased to have visited the assembly and that he has learned a great deal about all of the people who work in the school community. Now make the squeaking noise again and hold the gingerbread man to your ear.)

Oh, the gingerbread man has a question for the children now. He wants to know if any of you are good at running, as he has a special message for all the fast runners…

> **Run, run, as fast as you can**
> **You can't catch me**
> **I'm the gingerbread man!**

Well, we'll see about that, gingerbread man! I'm going to put you back in my bag now before you escape!

Reflection

When the gingerbread man jumped out of the oven and ran off, he met lots of people and animals along the way. As we move around the school, we meet a great many people who are here to help us in different ways. As we are all together now in the same place, I think it would be a really good idea it we all gave them a big thank-you for the work they do to make our school a safe, happy place for everybody.

The bundle of sticks

 Focus

This assembly investigates the advantages of a cohesive group.

 You will need

A pile of A4 scrap paper (about 30 sheets); calming music (such as Bach or Mozart).

 Opening

Choose a volunteer from the audience and ask him/her to tear the whole pile of paper in one go. It's very hard to tear through a pile of paper! Choose another volunteer and repeat the challenge. Carry on choosing volunteers until half a dozen have come forward. Ask these children to remain at the front while you read a story.

▶▶ Development

Now read Aesop's fable 'The Bundle of Sticks'.

A man had many fine sons but they were always arguing with one another. He tried to tell them that they must learn to work together, but they just carried on quarrelling.

One day, the father called his sons into the yard and showed them a big bundle of sticks. He called to his eldest son and asked him to snap the bundle in two. Then he called the second son and asked him to do the same thing. Each son huffed and puffed and tried with all of his strength but not one of them could even bend the bundle.

Then the father sighed and untied the string that held the bundle together. He separated the sticks and gave one stick to each of his sons.

'Now try,' he said. Each son took one stick and broke it easily.

Then the father said, 'My sons, if you stop arguing and learn to work together you will be as strong as this bundle of sticks. But if you are divided among yourselves, you will be broken as easily as you have broken the sticks. You need to be united and support one another if you want to be strong.'

Ask if anyone has a suggestion that might help the volunteers to tear the pile of paper. Now divide the paper among your volunteers. Count 'One, two, three, tear!' and see if the job is easier. Extend the concept of group strength by talking about the amount of adult teamwork that is required to run a school. List all the members of staff one by one and ask if the children know what special contributions each adult makes. Don't forget the cleaners and other members of staff who work while the children are not in school. (Ideally, you might be able to invite staff to attend the assembly and speak for themselves.) Close this part of the assembly by asking the children to identify activities that are only fun when they are done together as a group (such as football, drama, problem-solving, dancing…)

⚘ *Reflection*

Beautiful music can only be made if all the players work together as a team. Beautiful music can only be heard if everyone in the audience is considerate, sits still and listens quietly.

Play the calming music and let the children listen until a meditative atmosphere is achieved.

Two plus two can make five!

Focus

We can share all our skills and talents for the benefit of everyone.

You will need

A tin of milk powder; jug of water; a chocolate flake; strawberries or other fruit; a liquidiser; a picture of a sports team winning a tournament.

Opening

Begin by asking for four volunteers to hold up the milk powder, jug of water, fruit and chocolate flake.

Which ones do you like best? I think some of these items appear to be a bit more attractive or 'better' than the others. Do you think this seems fair? I've got a way of making sure that everybody gets some chocolate and fruit so that nobody is left with just a jug of water!

In front of the children, put all four items into a liquidiser to make a milkshake. Explain that some of these ingredients might seem more attractive than the others, but all of them are needed in order to make a delicious milkshake. (This is why you need to use milk powder and water. Milk is quite tasty on its own but you need to have a mix of 'nice' and 'not so appealing but necessary' ingredients if you are to make the point that ALL talents are useful to the team.)

▶▶ Development

We all have talents. Can anyone tell me about any special talents they have?

Ask for contributions from the assembly. Point out that some people have talents that are not so obvious – some quiet people may be very good listeners and will notice lots of little details, for example.

When I made the milkshake I used a variety of ingredients to make something that was nice for everybody. There are many things that are like that in life, where it takes a group or team to make something special.

Hold up a picture of a winning team and talk about how it needs a whole group of people to share their talents to achieve. Point out what individual members of the team might do. Talk about projects that are happening in school and emphasise that these too are due to the efforts of groups of people who work together and share their talents.

⌐⌐ *Reflection*

If everybody shares their talents and works together we can make this school a wonderful place. We can fill it with beautiful pictures and writing and science and maths projects and enjoy all of our lessons. We will have great sports days and tidy classrooms. We will have classes where nobody feels left out because everyone will know that their talent will come in useful and be appreciated.

Taking care

 Focus

We need to look after the equipment we use so that everyone can share the things they need to work and play happily.

 You will need

A few bright examples of children's artwork; four felt-tipped pens (blue, green, red and black).

 Opening

Share some examples of the children's artwork with the assembly. Talk about what makes them so good and how we all like to see wonderful pictures and take them home to show our families. Ask the children what sort of things we need to make such lovely pictures. Take suggestions. Use the following script:

Yes, we need paper, pens, paints and ideas. But what happens if we go to paint a picture and find that the paints have dried up, the brushes are ruined, the paper is crumpled or the pens are broken? How do we feel?

Now point to the teacher who has the job of making sure that every class has plenty of paper and pens. Explain that she needs to make sure that we have enough money to pay for all the things that we use and have to replace, and sometimes worries about this.

▶▶ Development

Watch me do this finger rhyme and join in when you have got the hang of it.

> **Four felt pens sitting in a tray**
> **We're doing colouring in today** (make circular movements with the blue pen)
> **The blue one was hidden** (put it in your pocket)

Where no-one could see (put hand over eyes and look around)
So nobody found it (shake head from side to side)
And then there were three.

Three felt pens sitting in a tray
We're doing colouring in today (use green pen)
The green one was broken
And snapped right through (pretend to snap pen)
No one could use it
So then there were two.

Two felt pens sitting in a tray
We're doing colouring in today (use black pen)
The black one was dropped (drop the pen)
Hit the floor, came undone (point to the floor)
So then there was one.

One felt pen sitting in the tray
We're doing colouring in today (use red pen)
The red one got lost (hide pen in your sleeve)
Where has it gone? (look mystified)
Nobody found it
So then there were none.

No felt pens sitting in the tray
We can't do colouring in today.

Mrs Smith would be feeling a bit worried on a day like this! When things aren't looked after properly, they need to be replaced over and over again. When we come to use something, we need to think of the next person who will need it and look after it properly.

Ask for the children's suggestions about ways classroom equipment might be damaged.

☁ *Reflection*

Each of us has enjoyed making and looking at the beautiful pictures that we've shared today. We all want to make more and more wonderful artworks. It's important to remember that we must look after the things that we need to use when we are creating our pictures. But we need to look after everything around us, because we share it with everyone else.

Get sorted

 Focus

Time is precious so don't waste it.

You will need

A selection of classroom equipment organised in containers; a collection of junk/useless items; a large box; a table.

Opening

Before the assembly, you will need to fill a large box with a mixture of classroom equipment and junk objects. Arrange the other classroom equipment (organised in containers) neatly on the table. Tell the children that you will be playing a game to see who can be the quickest to collect a number of things. Ask for two volunteers: one must use the box and the other must use the items on the table. Give them a series of tasks, such as:

Find me three things that we need if we are going to write a story.
Bring me five things that we use in maths lessons.
Fetch four things that we use in art lessons.

⏩ *Development*

When you have done this task a few times, ask the assembly which child was able to find the necessary items with the greater ease. Can anyone explain why there was a difference in their search times? Was this a fair game? Why not?

For everyone to be able to save time, we all need to be able to find things quickly when we look in the place where they belong. We can give everyone a gift of time by making sure we put everything back in its place. Being organised makes life easier for us all.

Reflection

Schools are places where you learn. Your teachers and parents want you to learn as much as possible while you are there. We have just seen how much time is lost if we have to search for things that have not been properly organised or cared for. Responsibility means 'to take care of'. Everyone has a responsibility to take care of the things that we need each day and to put them back in the right place.

Getting on and falling out

Working together and playing together is not always easy, as every school knows. There are rules and codes to help everyone get along, but there are also social skills that need to be developed as we grow. This section looks at friendship and how we can work together as a group to help to solve conflicts when things go wrong.

'What's on the menu?' explores the qualities that we look for in a friend – what do we want from a friend and what can we give? It also asks children to consider the characteristics that we don't really want!

Appreciating and accepting another's point of view is an important part of getting along as a community. 'The way I see it' and 'The caucus race' give clear illustrations of the difference between fact and opinion. Children can begin to appreciate that even though people don't always see things in the same way we can respect their views.

Of course, things don't always go to plan. There are bad days and good days and, much of the time, a mix of both! You can use 'The rough with the smooth' to help children to look for the positive points in a situation and take a level-headed view when things are less than perfect.

'Break friends, make friends' uses a story from the Bible to explore the theme of forgiveness. Everyone spurned Zacchaeus, but Jesus took the time to focus on the good in him which led to a new start for everyone.

This section closes with a reminder of those little phrases that help any group to work together – those rules and guidelines that can help stop disputes before they begin. 'A few of my useful things' will deliver the message that rules have an important function and can make life easier for all.

What's on the menu?

 Focus

To investigate the qualities we look for in our friends.

 You will need

A chef's hat and an apron; a table; two chairs; notebook and pencils; flip-chart; microphone (it doesn't need to work).

 Opening

Choose a confident child, dress him/her as a chef and introduce him/her to the assembly as the latest celebrity chef. Choose another child to be an interviewer for a cookery programme that is devising a new menu for a restaurant. Help them to ask questions such as 'Why does the chef cook prune and frogs' legs pancakes?', 'How does he/she decide what goes on the menu?' and 'Is customer feedback important? Why?'

Write some ideas for the new menu on the flip-chart and ask the children which items they would select. Thank the chef and the interviewer and send them back to their places.

 Development

Just as we can choose food from a menu, we can also choose our friends.

Ask for the children's help in making a 'menu' of qualities that we like/want when we get to know people. Use the flip-chart to make a list of desirable qualities – loyalty, sharing, kindness and so on. Now make a list of things that would be 'off the menu' – spitefulness, jealousy, lying etc.

Does anyone know what happens if a customer in a restaurant is unhappy with their dinner? What would they do if they were served unhealthy food? Friendships are even more important and we have the right to choose our

30

friends with just as much care. There is an important difference though. Friendship is a two-way thing. We want our friends to be kind, loyal and so on, but we need to make sure that we are also being a good friend to people around us. Friendship is as old as humanity itself. The following poem is very, very old but it makes as much sense today as it did hundreds of years ago.

OATH OF FRIENDSHIP

I want to be your friend
For ever and ever without break or decay.
When the hills are all flat
And the rivers are all dry,
When it lightens and thunders in winter
When it rains and snows in summer,
When heaven and earth mingle
Not till then will I be parted from you.

Anonymous, China, 1st century BC

Reflection

Help us all to be good friends to one another. Help us to be loyal and to never let each other down. Good friends never talk badly behind one another's back or say mean things about each other. Good friends share things with each other and support each other when one of them is unhappy or unlucky. Help us to be better friends, even when it is difficult, because friendship is one of the most important things in our world.

The way I see it

 Focus

To encourage respect for differing points of view.

 You will need

A large box: draw something different on each of the four vertical faces, such as a black square, a picture of a horse, a yellow star, a blue circle; a black plastic bin-liner; a low table.

 Opening

Put the box inside the plastic bag so that nobody can see it. Place the table in the middle of the hall so that the children can sit all around it. Take the bag to the centre of the hall, put it on the table and remove the bag. Point to children facing different parts of the box and ask them what they can see on the box from where they are sitting.

You can all see very different things, can't you? What you can see depends on where you are sitting. Nobody is 'wrong'. You can see things from your position. We call this your viewpoint, standpoint or point of view.

▶ Development

Role-play a situation that demonstrates that there are often many different viewpoints about the same thing. You may want to think about a scenario that is relevant to your particular setting, or use the following example:

In Rainbow Street there are four houses.

Mrs Yellow lives in number One. She is very old and she finds it hard to walk all the way to the High Street to get her shopping.

Mr and Mrs Green live in number Two with their four children, Arthur, Aiden,

Alan and Alex. They are all mad about football.

Mr Blue lives in number Three. He is an artist and he likes to paint the view from his house.

Miss Red lives in number Four. Her hobby is swimming but she hates having to drive 20 miles to the nearest swimming pool.

Across the road from the four houses there is a big empty field. One day a man came to Rainbow Street and knocked on each door. He asked the people inside what they would like the Council to do with the big empty field.

Ask for suggestions (or role-play) points of view that might be expressed by each household.

Tell the children that this story doesn't have an ending yet. The man from the council wrote down everyone's point of view in a big notebook and he has promised to let them know soon. They are all waiting for the postman.

What do you think the council will decide? Has the council got an easy job or a hard job to decide between the choices of people with such different points of view? Imagine what their job would be like if there were 20 houses in Rainbow Street!

Thank the children for all their different contributions and different points of view.

⟁ *Reflection*

Every single person in the world is different from every other person. Some people are rich and some people are poor. Some people live as part of a family with brothers and sisters and some people are 'only' children. Some people are old and some people are just little tiny babies in their pushchairs. Every one of us has a different way of looking at the world. Each of us has our own very special point of view. We should try to listen to everyone's point of view and help them to listen to our point of view. We can live together peacefully and happily.

The caucus-race

 Focus

To understand the difference between fact and opinion and see how this knowledge has a positive effect on social interaction.

 You will need

A large red square; a collection of familiar objects in unusual designs to provoke strong opinions; flip-chart.

 Opening

Hold up the red square. Tell the children that you are going to say three things about it. Ask them to listen carefully to each point.

Here is a square. The square is red. Red squares are better than blue squares.

Now ask for a show of hands at your questions.

Is this is a square? (This is a fact so everybody should agree.)
The square is red. (Again, everybody should agree.)
Red squares are better than blue squares. (Point out that the first two sentences are statements of fact. We can't argue about these statements because they are statements of truth and that is why everybody put up their hand. The third statement is an opinion. This means that it might be someone's personal viewpoint and that means that other people might well have a different opinion.)

Hold up a second object and ask for factual statements about it. Write these facts on the flip chart under the heading 'facts'. Now ask the children to give their opinions. Write these on the flipchart and discuss the range of opinions that have been expressed. Point out that sometimes we hold strong opinions but, at other times, we can have no strong feelings on a subject.

⏩ *Development*

Facts are about truth. Opinions are more personal and are about how we feel about something, whether we think it is right or wrong or good or bad. That makes them personal. We need to agree about facts but we can all have different opinions.

Sometimes we get into situations where we need to think carefully about things that have happened to us. We need to think about what actually happened and find out the facts before we can decide about our opinion.

There is a story about a creature who had to do such a thing in a famous book called 'Alice in Wonderland'. Alice met a very strange animal called the Dodo. He was sitting with a lot of other curious creatures when the Dodo decided that they should all have a caucus-race. This is what happened.

'What is a caucus-race?' said Alice; not that she much wanted to know, but the Dodo had paused as if it thought that *somebody* ought to speak, and no one else seemed inclined to say anything.

'Why,' said the Dodo, 'the best way to explain it is to do it.'

First it marked out a racecourse, in a sort of circle ('The exact shape doesn't matter,' it said), and then all the party were placed along the course, here and there. There was no 'One, two, three, and away!' but they began running when they liked, and left off when they liked, so that it was not easy to know when the race was over. However, when they had been running for half an hour or so, the Dodo suddenly called out 'The race is over!' and they all crowded round it, panting, and asking, 'But who has won?'

This question the Dodo could not answer without a great deal of thought, and it sat for a long time with one finger pressed upon its forehead while the rest waited in silence. At last the Dodo said, '*Everybody* has won, and all must have prizes.'

In the story, it was the Dodo's opinion of the facts that decided who had won the race. What were the facts? Everyone started from a different position on the track, there was no finishing line, everyone started at different times. In the Dodo's opinion, this meant that everyone had won.

Ask the children for their opinions about the race. Was it a good race? Would they have liked to take part? Do they think it was fair? Close the discussion by asking the children to suggest occasions when it is necessary to be very sure about the facts before we form an opinion and decide how to act. (For example, in police investigations, if you are a doctor, if there is a fight in the playground.)

Reflection

Facts are important things. When there is a problem, we need to know the facts if we are going to sort things out fairly and make things right. Opinions are important too and we all have a right to hold opinions of our own. We must learn to respect the fact that other people's opinions may be different from ours.

The rough with the smooth

Focus

When things go wrong we can look for the positive to make matters better.

You will need

Something rough like sandpaper and something smooth like velvet; a list of the little things that can go wrong at school and some that can go right, for example, 'I spilt water all over my painting' or 'I got a star for my story' (write the examples on pieces of paper, fold them up and put them in a hat).

Opening

Ask for a volunteer to come up and, stroke the sandpaper and describe how it feels against their skin: rough. Ask for another volunteer to feel the velvet and describe the sensation.

Life can be a bit like sandpaper and velvet – sometimes it is rough and irritating, and sometimes it is smooth and feels good. Listen to this poem and think about whether the writer is having a rough day or a smooth day.

Tuesday morning
My writing was smudgy
My sums were all wrong
I lost my new pencils
I couldn't sing the song.

When we had to choose partners
I was left to the end
Because nobody wants me
As their special friend.

When we went in for dinner
I was last in the queue
So the pizzas were finished
And I had to have stew.

Then I tripped and fell over
When we went out to play
I'll be glad when it's over
I DON'T LIKE TODAY!

▶▶ Development

Now ask the children if they agree that it was definitely a rough day with no smooth bits. Or was it? Now read the rest of the poem.

Tuesday afternoon
I liked doing science
Miss gave me a star
And said, "What a clever,
Hard worker you are!"

Then I sat next to Josie
We made models with clay
So how has my day been?
My day's been okay!

Ask the assembly if anyone has had a day like that when nothing seems to go right. Has anyone had a day when EVERYTHING seemed to go right? Make a comment on the difference in the show of hands.

Most days are a bit like a mixture of sandpaper and velvet – a bit of rough and a bit of smooth. Not many days are all bad but sometimes it can feel that way. Sometimes it can feel much worse than it actually is. We have to remember to enjoy the good things and find ways to improve the bad things. Enjoying the good things isn't hard work but all of us could do with a little help to make the bad things better.

Ask for volunteers to come forward and take a slip of paper out of the hat. If they pull out an example of a good thing for a 'smooth' day, they should receive a clap. If they choose a 'rough' thing they should receive some advice from the other children that might make them feel better (they can use the prompt 'Would it help if...')

⌬ *Reflection*

Every day has some smooth and some rough and we need to remember not to lose our tempers even when people and things make us cross. We must try to keep our patience when things don't go right, and not to lose hope when things are difficult: we need to learn how to take the rough with the smooth.

Break friends, make friends

 Focus

To investigate the power of forgiveness.

 You will need

A flip-chart.

 Opening

Ask the children for their definitions of 'forgiveness'. Make a list of these on the flipchart.

Some things are easier to forgive than others, especially if the person is truly sorry. This is a story about someone who was unpopular because he knew exactly what he was doing and didn't seem to care who he hurt.

When Jesus lived in Palestine his homeland wasn't ruled by his own people. It was ruled by another country. A huge Roman army had marched into Palestine and conquered it many years before and the people had to serve the Romans and do as they were told.

Every family in Palestine had to pay taxes to the Romans and all that money was taken to Rome. The Romans didn't collect the taxes themselves but employed local people to do it. The people hated paying their taxes but they hated the tax collectors even more. The man they hated most was Zacchaeus because he not only collected taxes for the Romans but he overcharged his neighbours and made lots of money for himself. Nobody ever spoke to Zacchaeus except to shout at him and tell him to go away. Nobody wanted to be his friend.

One day, Jesus came to the town where Zacchaeus lived. Zacchaeus wanted to

go and hear Jesus speak but he had to be careful because he might be cursed or shouted at if anyone saw him in the crowd. So he quietly climbed a tree and watched as Jesus spoke to the crowd. All the people from the town were there and they all wanted to invite Jesus back to their homes for a rest and a meal.

'Come and eat at my house, Jesus,' said one.

'Have a rest at mine,' said another.

But Jesus politely turned down every invitation. He looked around the crowd and then he called out, 'Zacchaeus, Zacchaeus, come down from that tree. I'm tired and I'm hungry and I'm coming to your house for supper.'

Zacchaeus was so astounded he nearly fell out of the tree but the crowd was angry.

'He's a thief,' they shouted.

'He steals all of our money,' they yelled. 'How could you even think about sitting down with such a horrible man?'

'A holy man should eat with good honest people,' they declared.

⏩ Development

We don't know what Jesus and Zacchaeus talked about. But we do know what Zacchaeus did soon after Jesus had left the city. Can you guess? Yes, he gave all of his money to the poor and needy. Who thinks that they can guess what Jesus might have said?

Ask the children to help you to make a list of the things they look for in a friend.

Sometimes we fall out with our friends. Without mentioning any names, can anyone think of the reasons why people fall out and stop being friends? Does anyone have any suggestions for ways in which friends can get together again? (Talk things through, forgive and forget.)

💭 Reflection

We all need good friends. Good friends make our lives happy and look after us. Good friends share their toys and listen to us when we need to talk. Zacchaeus was a mean, greedy man who took money from his neighbours. He had no friends and was very lonely until Jesus was kind to him and befriended him. Then Zacchaeus felt warm inside and changed his ways. He became a kind, generous caring man and felt much happier. We should be good friends to other people and try to see the good in them.

A few of my useful things

Focus

To consider the function of rules and why it is important that rules are kept.

You will need

A selection of unusual but useful things: look around your kitchen/garage/cupboards and find some gadgets that the children may not have seen before, such as a paperweight, soap dish, camping stove, curling tongs; a set of your school/classroom rules (each written on a card).

Opening

Choose a volunteer to come up and choose one of the useful objects. Ask them to show it to the audience, describe it and try to deduce what it does and why it is useful. Tell the children a little story about each gadget. Even if you have to exaggerate a bit, stress why you find it useful and why you have decided to keep it and not throw it away. Continue with the other items until all have been found to be useful and worth keeping.

⏩ Development

Today we've found some things that are useful and that means they are worth keeping. I've brought another set of useful things with me today and I'm going to show them one at a time and ask you why they might be worth keeping.

You will need your school rules. Ask for volunteers to come forward and hold up one rule at a time. Read the rule and ask for suggestions about why it is important, useful and worth keeping.

Reflection

We all have many useful things at home and in our classrooms. They are things that we need to help us to get our work done without wasting lots of time and make life much easier. Rules are useful because they help us to live and work together without getting into problems and difficulties. They help us to get along together. When we keep the rules, we are able to play games together and help the school to run smoothly. Rules make everyone feel safe and happy, so let's remember to keep them.

46

Say no to bullying

These assemblies will reinforce approaches to the prevention of bullying. They help children to empathise with how it feels to be bullied and to offer kindness when they find bullying happening to others. Strategies are suggested to deal with the situation of peer-group pressure and promote a 'telling culture' where problems are not kept secret.

The story of Cinderella ('Fairy godmothers') offers plenty of opportunity to discuss issues relating to bullying, and it is used here to encourage all children to understand that they can take a role to help others feel better. 'You don't scare me, Mr Lion' and 'What would you do?' will help children to deal confidently with bullying situations.

Fairy godmothers

 Focus

Telling a grown-up about bullying or negative behaviour is the best way of helping others.

 You will need

A copy of the traditional tale 'Cinderella' (you may not have time to read this in the assembly, so it's a good idea to ask the other teachers to read it to the children in class in the days before the assembly); a fairy godmother costume (something simple – a plain apron decorated with tinsel and stars is fine); a 'magic' wand; large safety pins; flip-chart and pens.

 Opening

When dealing with bullying, every school needs to promote a 'telling environment' because problems cannot be solved if they are kept secret.

People can be unkind in many ways. Calling people names and making insulting remarks is one. Spreading nasty stories and excluding others from activities is another. It might not seem so direct as calling names, but it can make people really unhappy. The story of Cinderella features all sorts of unkind and bullying behaviour. Who knows the story of Cinderella? Weren't those ugly sisters nasty and unkind? Who can tell me some of the unkind things that they did to Cinderella?

Take suggestions from the floor and repeat them. For example, 'Yes, Cinderella wasn't her real name. They just called her Cinders or Cinderella, didn't they?' Give prompts if the children get stuck.

Until Cinderella met her fairy godmother, her life seemed sad and lonely. But then she was able to go to the ball and meet new people. Then she was happy again. I expect we were all pleased when we got to that part of the story.

▶ *Development*

Fairy godmothers seem like very interesting people. Have any of you ever had one? Well now's your chance to see what it might be like. Can I have a volunteer to be the fairy godmother?

Ask a volunteer to come to the front. Give them your fairy godmother costume to wear, and hand them the wand.

Who can tell me something about a fairy godmother's job?

Take suggestions from the floor but help the children to see that a fairy godmother helps people who are unhappy.

All of us might feel lonely and unhappy sometimes and we would like to have a fairy godmother to make us feel happy again. I'm afraid that sometimes a few of us might behave like those nasty ugly sisters and call people names or not let others join in our fun. I know that we can't do magic tricks and turn pumpkins into carriages but we can help others by listening and caring for each other. We can also try to make things better for people who are being treated unkindly. Every one of you can be a fairy godmother in your own way. If you notice that someone is being treated unkindly what do you think that you should do?

Again, take suggestions and repeat those that have value. List these on the flip-chart under the heading 'Ways to be a fairy godmother'.

☁ *Reflection*

Sometimes a few people can be unkind and act like the ugly sisters in Cinderella. Sometimes children are made to feel sad and lonely and hurt. If you see something like that going on, you need to think about what the fairy godmother would do. You can wave your magic wand and go and find a grown-up and tell them what you have seen. Telling someone about unkind behaviour is the best way to make everyone safe.

You don't scare me, Mr Lion

 Focus

To look at strategies for facing our fears.

 You will need

A container and a list of common childhood fears (the dark, monsters, spiders etc); some slow, calm music.

 Opening

Ask the children some questions that require a 'yes' or 'no' response.

If you were a mouse, would you be afraid of an elephant?
Well, you wouldn't need to be because elephants are vegetarian and afraid of mice!

If you were a butterfly, would you be afraid of a great white shark?
Well, you wouldn't need to be because sharks live in the sea and never come to the land where butterflies live.

If you were a hare, would you be afraid of a lion?
Well, you might be but I know of one who wasn't and this is his story.

Read the story of 'The Hare, the Lion, the Man and his Dogs' (from a collection by Frank Worthington).

One day, a man who was a big chief called to his dogs and said, 'Come on, we are going to hunt antelope'.

And the man and his dogs went out to hunt antelope.

And when they had killed some antelope and the sun was very hot, the

50

man carried the antelope into a cave and sat down.

And the dogs also went into the cave.

And then Lion went into the cave and sat down.

And after Lion came Hare, and he sat down too.

And Lion said, 'Man, let the dogs eat the antelope, and then you shall eat the dogs, and after that I will eat you.'

But the man was very angry and said, 'Who is it who eats a dog?' Then the Lion said, 'Do not argue with me. Let the dogs eat the antelope, then you, Man, shall eat the dogs, and after that I, Lion, will eat you.'

Then Hare said, 'Yes, Man, agree with Lion quickly, let the dogs eat the antelope, then you must eat the dogs, then Lion will eat you, and after that, I, Hare shall eat Lion.'

But Lion said, 'No, I do not agree. How can Hare, who is so little, eat me, when I am so big?'

So Lion ran after Hare, but Hare ran away. The Lion came back into the cave and sat down.

And after that Hare came back also and he sat down.

Then said Lion, 'Man, let the dogs eat the antelope, then you must eat the dogs, and after that, I, Lion, will eat you.'

But the man again refused.

Then Hare said to the man, 'You must agree, Man, and you must agree quickly, for the sun will soon be gong down and I, Hare, have far to go to get to my home. Now, Man, let the dogs eat antelope, then you, Man, must eat the dogs, and after that Lion will eat you, then I, Hare, will eat Lion.'

And Lion was very angry with Hare and again ran after him. But Hare again ran away and he hid himself in some very thick bushes.

The Lion began to hunt for Hare. And Lion looked here and he looked there. For a long time Lion searched for Hare; but because Hare was a little fellow, and because the bushes were very thick, Lion could not find him.

And Lion said, 'Where is that fellow Hare?'

But Hare did not answer Lion.

And Lion called to Hare and said, 'Hare, come out! Come out, Hare!'

But Hare did not answer Lion; he remained in the very thick bushes.

And because of all his hunting for Hare and because the sun was very hot, Lion became tired and went back to the cave.

And when Lion came to the cave, he found that the man had gone to his home and had taken with him the antelope and his dogs.

And Lion was very sorry because he was hungry.

But the man, who was a big chief, gave Hare a village to live in because, he said, 'Hare has saved me from Lion'.

⏩ Development

Well, the hare has obviously found a way to beat his fear of lions. He is a very clever hare! Who can tell me about the clever plan he made to beat Lion? He stayed calm and thought of a way to solve the problem.

Take answers from the audience. Ask for volunteers to come up and take a piece of paper from the container.

This piece of paper says that some people are afraid of (insert a fear here). Who has a suggestion for helping someone to be brave about that fear?

Take suggestions from the audience and give prompts if necessary.

💭 Reflection

When we are afraid, we often start to breathe faster. If we make an effort to slow down our breathing, we feel ourselves getting calmer and more in control of things. When we feel calm and in control it is easier to find a solution to a problem.

Play the music and ask the children to become aware of their breathing. Ask them to practise slowing it down and making it strong and regular, creating a sense of calm control.

What would you do?

 Focus

To address peer-group pressure by developing refusal skills and ways of saying 'no'.

 You will need

A copy of the poem below.

 Opening

Read the poem 'When Joseph Brown Said' to the assembly.

When Joseph Brown said,
'Let's go and play in the woods,'
I didn't want to go.
But Tina and Jay said they were going,
So I went too.

When Joseph Brown said,
'Let's make a fire,'
I was scared.
But Tina and Jay went looking for sticks,
So I helped them.

When Joseph Brown said,
'Let's make it really big.'
I was afraid.
But Tina and Jay said, 'Yes, let's,'
So I said, 'Yes' too.

Later, when Mum asked me,
'Where've you been all day?'
I started crying.

Because Joseph Brown said
I'm not to tell anyone
Or he won't be my friend.

Now talk about the things that happen in the poem and how the child is feeling in each verse.

What is the word that he/she needs to learn to say?
(Ask the children for suggestions – you should get 'It's NO!')

It's a word that needs to be said sometimes. Has anyone got any suggestions to explain why this child doesn't say it?

▶ *Development*

Sometimes we can get into difficulties and troubles if we always do just what people ask us to. It's important to keep safe and out of trouble, so we need to learn to stop and think when someone asks us to do something. We need to think about what might happen. Sometimes NO is a very hard word to say, but we are all going to look at some ways to make it easier.

Model the positive body language which will help to show that you mean it when you say 'no' to something: standing tall, head up and making eye contact. Ask for confident volunteers to come up, one by one, and give them prompts. For example, 'Go and pull Miss Green's hair' or 'Let's mess up Susie's picture'. Encourage them to demonstrate a really assertive 'no', or 'no, thank you'. Ask all the children to stand up and say, 'No' or 'No, thanks' very firmly. Explain that sometimes we might need to say 'no' over and over. Demonstrate this with a volunteer.

'Let's pull Marie's hair.'
'No.'
'Oh, go on.'
'No, I'm not going to.'
'We'll only do it once.'
'No, I won't do it.'

'But it will be funny.'
'NO.'

One way to say no is to give reasons for your decision: 'No, I don't want to get into trouble,' or 'No, because it would make me feel bad'. Sometimes it helps to give the behaviour a name (stealing, bullying, being unkind, dishonest, breaking the rules). You might say, 'No, I won't do that because it's cheating/stealing/naughty' or something similar. You can also change the subject: 'I saw a good programme on TV yesterday' or 'How is your pet rabbit getting on?', for example.

Give more volunteers some scenarios so that they can demonstrate these skills, or you could ask the whole assembly to 'repeat after you'. Older children may like to learn to ask questions, such as 'Why do you think that is a good thing to do?' or 'Why would you want me to do something like that?' Tell the children that they can always just walk away or ask an adult to assist them. Finally, return to the poem and re-read it. Point out that, sometimes, we have to accept that someone is not a good friend. We need to make an important choice to stop being friends with that person and seek out those who make good choices and know how to be trustworthy companions.

⌔ *Reflection*

Sometimes, life is easy and everything goes well. Sometimes good friends surround us and we have happy times together. But sometimes we need to remember that 'no' is a word that can keep us safe. 'No' is a word that can help us to stay out of trouble. When we are asked to do things that are unkind or dangerous, we need to remember that we have the right to say 'no' and we have lots of different ways to say it clearly.

Going for goals

Motivation and development of the desire to follow a goal is addressed in this section. Setting goals will help children along the road to taking responsibility for their own success. But the path to any goal needs persistence and the ability to cope with frustration on the long journey and the problems that can get in the way.

Goals are often distant and success doesn't happen overnight. 'One step at a time' and 'Treasure seekers' help children to see that they should never be overwhelmed by what they have to do. Tiny steps are all it takes to find the treasure... every one gets you nearer!

Goals are useful in all sorts of situations. 'The best possible plan' demonstrates that having a goal can help you get round a problem. The Greek myth of Odysseus and the Cyclops is used here to introduce thinking skills that will help children work through difficulties and find solutions.

Finally, 'Look before you leap' examines consequences – what might happen when the goal is reached?

One step at a time

Focus

We need to have the patience to learn things step by step if we are to reach our goals.

You will need

A cassette player with a suitable piece of dance music; a colleague to assist; a collection of books of varying reading difficulty.

Opening

Invite a small group of volunteers to come forward and then lead the assembly with the following script.

Today I want you to learn a dance. It's hard to learn a dance all at once but I've got a special way to make it easier. I want all the dancers to stand in a circle as far away from me as you can. We are going to learn each move of the dance one step at a time.

As the children master each move, ask them to take one step closer to you. Give praise and encouragement at every move forward. Use the following steps:

1) *March on the spot.* (When this is mastered, give praise and ask the children to take a step towards you.)

2) *Punch the air with your hands.* (Give praise, and invite them to take another step towards you).

3) *Turn around once and jump in the air.*

4) *Crouch down and leap up.*

5) *Sit down still facing me in a circle.*

When your dancers have learned all the moves and are sitting close to you, play the music for the dance and repeat the steps to see how it looks.

58

⏩ *Development*

Didn't they do well! They learned the dance one step at a time and in the end they knew the whole dance. All learning is like that: we have to learn a little at a time. I'd like to show you another example. Mrs Brown, I saw you reading a book earlier today. Could you show it to the children?

Let your colleague show the book, pointing out the number of pages, lack of pictures, long words and so on.

Mrs Brown, you are obviously a very good reader. Have you always been able to read such difficult books?

Invite your colleague to explain her progress using the collection of books. For example:

When I started reading, I had books like this – with a few words and lots of pictures. Then I moved on to books with longer sentences. As I got better at reading, I had a favourite book that looked like this. Then I started liking books by a particular author. I read all of them. In the end, I was able to read big, long books like the one I was reading earlier.

💭 *Reflection*

Today, we watched some children learn a dance. They started off not knowing anything about it – not a single step. I expect they felt a bit nervous at first but they learned it a step at a time and in the end they danced beautifully. Everything that we do at school is like that dance. Some of you may worry that you'll never be able to read, write or do maths very well. You don't need to worry. Just think of moving along, one step at a time – because with every step you take, you will be moving towards your goal. Every small step forward is a step to be proud of.

Treasure seekers

Focus

How we can set and achieve our goals.

 ## You will need

A set of clues to make a treasure trail around the hall; a small prize (a bag of sweets or set of stickers); a list of stages needed to achieve good handwriting (see below).

 ## Opening

Before the assembly, plan out a simple treasure trail around the hall. Write a series of clues on card so that each one leads your volunteers to the next (eg 'Look inside the box under Mrs Green's chair'). Start the assembly by asking for volunteers to go on a special treasure trail. Give the children the first clue to read (they may need an adult helper). This will lead them to the location of the next clue. The other children can help if the group gets stuck. They should end up with a small parcel. Ask them to return to you and unwrap the package to reveal the treasure.

▶▶ Development

Our volunteers didn't get the treasure straight away. They had to work towards finding it. Life is like that too. We have to work hard and keep trying, until we get to where we want to be. But it is important that we know where it is we want to get to. If we don't know where we want to get to, then we will just wander around!

We call this our goal because it is just like scoring a goal in a football game. The ball goes from one player to another and is passed along, one move at a time, just like the trail moved from one clue to the next. When we think about what our goals for the year ahead might be, we need to think about it like a treasure trail and ask ourselves two important questions:

60

What are my goals for this year?

What will I need to do along the way to achieve my goals?

Ask the children if any of them have thought about what they would like to achieve this year. Have any of them decided to have good handwriting, for example? Ask these children to come to the front. Explain that the 'treasure' at the end of their trail is to have good handwriting. The clues (or stages) to achieve this will be:

Learning to hold a pencil properly.

Listening and watching their teacher demonstrate.

Concentrating on one letter at a time.

Being patient.

Practising at home.

Explain that every step along the way counts because every step takes us nearer to where we want to be.

💭 *Reflection*

Life is often like a treasure trail. We go from one thing to the next and, if we keep going, in the end we reach our goal and find the treasure that we have been searching for. We have many teachers and helpers to give us the clues that we need to keep us on the right path, making sure that we don't get lost and give up. Every step in the right direction is something to celebrate, and we are a school that celebrates everyone's achievements as they move towards their goals.

The best possible plan

 Focus

Looking at problems and taking positive steps to solve them.

 You will need

Flip-chart and pens.

 Opening

Sometimes we can come across a problem and think 'I don't know what to do. I'm stuck!' The problem is in the way and we have to stop and find a way get past it. But we don't have to sit there and wait for it to go away. We can work out ways to take a step at a time and work round the problem or solve it altogether. Today I'm going to tell about someone who lived a very long time ago in Ancient Greece. He was called Odysseus and he had a very big problem indeed.

Odysseus was a great hero of ancient Greece who went on an adventure that took him away from home for 20 years. During his long travels a terrible monster, called Polythemus, captured Odysseus and his men. Polythemus was a Cyclops, a kind of giant who has only one eye, right in the middle of his forehead.

For many days and nights, Odysseus and his men were trapped in a cave where Polythemus slept with his flock of sheep. Polythemus was so huge that he blocked the mouth of the cave and Odysseus and his men could not escape. The only time that he moved away was in the morning when he let his sheep out to graze and in the evening when he let them back in again.

Poor Odysseus! He felt so small and weak. When he looked at the sleeping giant he was afraid that he would never be able to escape and would never be able to get home.

▶▶ *Development*

Odysseus had a really big problem but he was a clever man who knew a lot about problem solving. Let's have a look at what he did.

Go to the flip-chart and write the heading 'problem'.

A problem has four main parts and Odysseus looked at all four of them very carefully. The first part is called the **setting***.* (Write the subheading 'setting'.) *This means that Odysseus looked at his situation very carefully so that he could see it clearly.*

Ask the children to help you to make a list of the context or setting of the problem: a cave, a hungry giant guarding the exit, some sheep let out to graze every morning.

The next thing he did was to think about his goal. (Write this subheading.) *That's easy! He wanted to escape and get home with his men.*

The third thing he did was to think about all that things that could go wrong. We call this the **obstacles***.*

Ask the children to help you to make a list of obstacles: Odysseus and his men might get too hungry and weak to do anything; the giant guards and sleeps at the exit; the giant is much bigger and more powerful than they are.

The fourth thing he did was to make a plan. Can any of you guess what it was?

Take suggestions from the floor and comment on the amount of thought that has gone into each one. If a child has heard the story of Odysseus and the Cyclops, don't worry, just commend them on their brilliant scheme and carry on taking suggestions. Finally, read the next part of the story which tells how Odysseus escaped and found freedom for his men, in his own words.

So there we were, trapped in the cave, fearing for our lives as the Cyclops roared in a rage that turned my blood to ice. How small and helpless I felt and

how terrified! All night long, I thought about my situation and tried to find a way to save my friends and myself. It was a matter of life and death and I had to think of something. But every plan seemed hopeless and I nearly gave up in despair.

Then I looked at the flock of sheep and had an idea. The sheep looked strong and healthy and were covered with thick black wool. I knew that Polythemus would let them out in the morning to roam around the island eating the grass. So I quietly stole some of the willow twigs that the Cyclops used for bedding and tied the sheep together in threes. I tied them like that so that each of my friends could be tied on to the middle sheep and have the ones on each side to protect him. I clung under the largest ram and waited for Polythemus to wake.

As soon as the sun rose, the sheep began to bleat and push towards the mouth of the cave. Polythemus counted them as they passed by but he didn't notice that my men were tied to their woolly chests.

When we were far enough away from the cave, I let go of my sheep and quickly untied my men. Then we all scrambled down to the beach and back to my ship. Everyone took their places at the oars and we sailed away as quickly as we could into the safety of the open seas.

If there is time you can reinforce the assembly by using the four stage model to consider problems that your children may have experienced – getting lost on the beach, losing a homework folder, name-calling and so on.

Reflection

Odysseus was strong and very good at fighting but what did he use to solve his problems? He used his brain. He was a great hero because he always stuck to the four stages of problem solving and used his thinking skills before he took action. Who can remember what the four stages are? Setting, goal, obstacles, plan.

Odysseus lived a very long time ago in Ancient Greece but we can learn from him and many other heroes and see how carefully they thought things through before deciding on their plan of action. The next time you have a problem, I want you to remember how Odysseus outwitted the giant Cyclops and remember that even though you might be small, you all have good thinking skills and will be able to escape from your own giants!

Look before you leap

 Focus

Considering the consequences of our actions.

 You will need

A flip-chart and a pen.

 Opening

Ask the children if they know what a proverb is. Tell them that not all learning comes from books or the internet or what people have written down. Some learning comes from experience: the things people have noticed and thought about. Proverbs didn't start in books. They have been called 'the wisdom of the street' because ordinary people thought them up a long time ago and we still use them today. List and explain a few proverbs:

A leopard can't change his spots

Still waters run deep

All work and no play makes Jack a dull boy

Two wrongs don't make a right

A stitch in time saves nine

Cut your coat according to your cloth

▶▶ Development

Sometimes, writers hear a good proverb and weave a story around it. I'm going to tell you a story like that.

There once lived two frog brothers called Freddie and Hoppy. They lived in a very nice pond at the end of Watery Lane and were very happy there until one hot summer when things went wrong. The sun shone every day and the rain stayed away. This was lovely for humans but not so good for frogs because

the water started to dry up and the pond became shallow. The frogs started to feel hungry and afraid.

Freddie and Hoppy decided that they had better have a look around and see if they could find somewhere wetter to live. So they hopped away from the pond at Watery Lane and started searching. They searched for hours and hours and then Hoppy came across an old well near Mr Bloggett's farm.

'That's just the place,' he cried, jumping onto the well. 'Come on, leap in! I'm desperate for a good swim.'

'No, no,' shouted Freddie. 'Wait.'

'But this is a perfect place for us,' said, Hoppy. 'What's the matter with you, Freddie? We're tired and we're dry and we're hungry.'

'No, no, no,' said Freddie. 'Wait a minute. Just look down the well and see how deep it is. We'd fall all the way down into the dark water at the bottom and never get out. Hoppy, remember to look before you leap!'

Ask the children if the story helped them to understand the proverb. Give them some situations when remembering the proverb might be useful. For example: someone asks you to go somewhere you're not sure about; you decide not to save up for a computer game but to spend your pocket money on sweets; you go out to play and leave your homework unfinished. Ask the children for suggestions of other situations when this proverb might come in useful.

💭 Reflection

Some kinds of knowledge are very old and have been passed down from generation to generation throughout the ages. Proverbs are the wisdom passed down to people over hundreds of years and show us that long, long ago people were thinking about life and coming to some very wise conclusions about things that can help us to make sensible decisions. Sometimes we need to think about what will happen before we make a decision. Sometimes we need to 'look before we leap'.

Good to be me

Positive self-awareness is the theme of the assemblies in this section, to help every child to feel special and valued. We all have a unique contribution to make to the world and these assemblies all celebrate this fact.

'Seed of a smile' looks to nature to remind us how we can all spread happiness and self-belief even on the greyest of days. The theme continues in 'Sunny side up'.

'Each and every one of us' introduces the school to 'the very special chair'. It might look extra special, draped in velvet, but underneath it's a chair just the like the ones in class. Everyone is sitting on an important chair every day, and everyone is special.

'Variety of life' and 'In the town of Trigatree' celebrate all the things that make us unique. These two assemblies, as well as 'For the reason that follows', encourage pride in our differences and confidence in our own voices.

'The air that we breathe' concludes the section with a focus on fitness and health.

The seed of a smile

 Focus

To show how we can scatter the seeds of self-belief and success.

 You will need

A range of different types of seed, and images or objects of autumn (golden coloured leaves, seeds, a warm scarf and so on).

 Opening

Introduce the subject of the seasons by explaining that many plants have something different to do during each season. Use this script:

Autumn is the season that plants get ready for the winter. One of the things that plants do is to make sure that their seeds are carried far and wide. Plants have many different ways of making sure that their seeds are able to find new places in which to grow.

Show the children the range of different seeds (or images) you have collected and explain some of the dispersal techniques that are used: wind blown (grass, dandelion); spread by animals (rose-hips, apples); burs and hooks (burdock).

Even a huge tree begins as a tiny seed. It starts off small and just keeps growing until it is big and strong.

▶▶ Development

A smile is like a little seed. The moment that you smile at someone, you put a little bit of happiness into the world that has everything that it needs to grow all by itself. We're going to play a little game now, to show you how this works. It's called 'Pass the smile'.

Invite some volunteers to stand up. Make eye contact with one child and smile.

Ask them to pass the smile to another child and then sit down. Continue until everyone is sitting down.

If we had time, we could have gone on and on until the whole school had passed on a smile. The smile would have gone on and on spreading just like the seeds in autumn. Everyone would be having that nice warm feeling that a smile brings with it. In fact, let's all have a smile at one another.

Tell the child at the end of each row to smile at the person next to them. Pass the smile down the row.

Good! See how the seed of a smile that we began with has spread throughout the whole school.

Reflection

Autumn can be a grey and wet time. The trees are losing their leaves and starting to look very bare. Night-time seems to come earlier and earlier in the afternoon and it is getting colder as winter comes closer. All the little seeds are hiding away under the earth and will wait until the spring before they start to grow. But, luckily for us, the seeds of happiness that we all call smiles can be spread around at any time of year. Smiles are sparkly and will brighten everyone up – even on a grey, wet day. So, let's all smile as much as we can and spread the sparkle of happiness around the school every day.

Sunny side up

Focus

Looking at moods and how we can make ourselves happier from day to day.

You will need

A book of jokes; a flip-chart.

Opening

Show the children the book of jokes and share a few of them. Tell the children that scientists have studied laughter, and what makes us laugh, and have decided that there are up to eleven things that can happen when we laugh.

We make a funny whooping noise

We open our mouth

The corners of our mouth get pulled up

Our nose scrunches up and wrinkles

We close our eyes

Crease lines appear all around our eyes

Tears sometimes fall from our eyes

We throw our head backwards

We raise our shoulders

Our tummy goes up and down

We hug our body

Ask for volunteers who can entertain or who know some jokes, or read a couple more examples from the book so that the children can see if the scientists are right.

Development

The same kind of scientists who studied laughter (called psychologists) have also looked at happiness in general. How do we know if someone is happy?

They might smile and look friendly for example.

Take suggestions from the assembly and make a list on the flip-chart.

What kind of things make us feel happy?

Ask for volunteers to describe what makes them happy.

Unfortunately, everybody feels sad sometimes. Does anyone have some good suggestions for 'cheering yourself up?'

Collect these on the flip chart as 'sadness busters' or 'happiness top tips'.

Scientists have studied happiness and they have some top tips to add to our list.

Always look on the bright side: 'It's wet play, we can't play football but I'm looking forward to drawing pictures with my friend.'

Don't expect too much – if we expect too much, we will be disappointed and it is much better to be pleasantly surprised when things go really well.

Add up lots of little 'happinesses' to make a big sense of happiness: 'We can't win the lottery everyday, but small, good, things happen to us all the time and we need to remember to notice these.'

Discuss each of these three elements of happiness to ensure that the children understand what you mean.

💭 *Reflection*

Sometimes we feel happy and sometimes we feel sad. Scientists are interested in what makes us feel different emotions and they have studied happiness because they want us to be happy as often as possible. If we are sad, we can find ways to cheer ourselves up. Often we are in charge of our own moods and can choose how we feel. When we are feeling fed up or sad, we need to remember that we can cheer ourselves up just by deciding to look at the sunny side of life.

Each and every one of us

Focus

Every one of us is a very special person.

You will need

An ordinary school chair draped with a piece of plush fabric.

Opening

Place the covered chair at the front of the hall, then use the following script to help you deliver the assembly.

Look at this very special chair. Do you like it? It's an important chair for a special person. Now let me see, is there anyone here who would like to come and sit on the special chair?

Choose a volunteer and invite them to come up and sit on the chair.

Sam is sitting on the important chair so he/she must be a very special person.

Make a fuss of the child: ask if they are comfortable; put a crown on their head; give them a plate of biscuits. This will help them feel important and get into role.

Who would like to ask this very important person a question?

Invite questions from the floor. If necessary, give some assistance: 'I expect that Sam has a favourite lesson. Does anyone want to ask him what it is?' Ensure that the children behave appropriately towards a very special person. Sum up the child's special qualities: 'Sam is a very special person. He likes writing stories, is interested in the Vikings, he has a new baby brother and a new pair of shoes!' If you have time, give other children a turn too. Then, look thoughtfully at the chair.

This important chair has allowed us all to get to know some very special children. But it hasn't had enough important children sitting on it. In fact, this is a hall filled with very special children because you are ALL wonderful and important and very special. Wait a minute! What's this? What's underneath this lovely cover? (Remove the plush material.)

Well, who would have thought it! This important chair is a school chair, the kind found in every classroom. That's good because it means that each one of you can sit on an important chair all day, every day. All the staff in the school know that every child here is important and now, when you sit down in your classroom, we want you to remember that you are sitting on your own 'important chair' and you are sitting on it because you ARE important.

⌒ *Reflection*

Conclude the assembly by reminding the children that each and every one of them is irreplaceable and important.

Each of you should feel proud to be the interesting person that you are. We treat important people with respect and thoughtfulness. All of you deserve to be treated like that, which means that we must all remember to be kind and considerate to one another.

The variety of life

Focus

To celebrate diversity and to be proud of who we are.

You will need

A wide selection of different books, or you may prefer to collect a wide variety of plants, or pictures or models of animals, fish, machines - any of these would work equally well; two life-size outlines of children (draw round a couple of volunteers before the assembly, cut round the outlines and pin these on to the wall).

Opening

Show the children your special collection. Ask for volunteers to come forward and present each one with something from the collection. Ask them to describe their item and what they like or don't like about it.

Is one kind of thing better than another? I don't think so, because the variety means that we can enjoy things for different purposes and in different ways.

Development

 Show the children the two outlines and give each one a name – but not the name of anyone in the school so that no-one can take this exercise personally. Ask the children to contribute different words to 'describe' and give a personality to each of the two outlines, for example:

Quiet/noisy

Sociable/private

Happy/sad

Good at sport/clumsy

Good at reading

Good at painting

And so on…

Ask two volunteers to stand at opposite ends of the room, each with an outline, and fill the space in between with a line of children.

Just as we need a huge a variety of books so that reading doesn't become boring, so we need a wide variety of people in the world. That is what makes people so interesting. It is not a question of better or best because we need all kinds of people to make the world go round.

What would happen if EVERYBODY was a great leader and nobody was a good follower?

What would happen if everyone was excellent at talking but nobody was good at listening?

What would the world be like if everyone was good at sport but no-one was good at sitting and thinking?

Use this opportunity to mention issues that are relevant to your setting and, with subtlety, help any child who is having a hard time at the moment – by celebrating a wide range of differences.

⊙ *Reflection*

We are all different and that means that we are all special. Help us to learn about each other and do all that we can to celebrate our special qualities. We are dependent on each other. Help us to work together so that peace and understanding and happiness can grow in our world. Help us not to be jealous of other people because they seem to be happier or more successful than we are. Help us not to look down on other people because we think we are better than they are. Help us to see that everyone has the right to be who they are and to be grateful for the wonderful variety of life.

In the town of Trigatree

 Focus

To develop awareness of cultural diversity.

 What you need

A selection of different clothes; examples or pictures of clothing from various cultures and times in history.

 Opening

Look out of the window and comment on the weather. Turn to the children and welcome some to your assembly: 'Hello Susie, you are looking warm in your sweater', 'Hi there, Christopher. I see that you are wearing your long grey trousers today,' and so on.

We all dress in ways that suit our needs but people dress in different ways. Take, for instance, the town of Trigatree. Now that is such an unusual place that someone has written a poem about it.

In the land of imagination
Is a town called Trigatree.
Their ducks say moo,
And their cows say quack.
Their cars are planes
And their homes are stars.
That may seem strange to you and me
But they like it that way in Trigatree.

Because the land of Trigatree lives in our imagination, we can dress the people in any way that we like.

Choose a volunteer to be a person from Trigatree and ask them to stand at the front. Give them a new name: Trig. Ask other children to choose a hat, cloak,

78

shoes and other items to dress Trig. Then ask Trig to give a bow and say 'hello' to everyone in Trigatree language.

 # Development

Ask the children a series of questions to investigate the different reasons for wearing particular kind of clothing: to suit the weather or climate, for special occasions, to suit their occupation or simply to look good. After each question see if the children can guess why Trig is wearing a particular item of clothing.

We need to wear different clothes in different seasons. Who can tell me about the clothes we wear in the winter but don't wear in the summer? Why do we do that? Can you tell just by looking if Trigatree is cold or hot today? How can you tell? Can we tell anything else about Trigatree from the clothes?

If you wish, you may like to allow the children to find out more about Trig's life and the culture of Trigatree. Let the children ask any questions they like and be ready to help Trig come up with some interesting answers. For example:

'Trig, do you have birthday parties?'
'No, we don't celebrate birthdays but the whole town has a huge party at the seaside on Midsummer Day.'

Show the children the pictures or examples of clothing from different cultures, times and places in the world and see if they can deduce anything from them about climate, work, lifestyle and so on. You can link these to current classroom topics.

 # Reflection

The world is a wonderful place and people live in every part of it. In some places it is very hot and people need to dress to keep cool. Elsewhere, it is cold and they need to wear heavy boots and coats to keep warm. We sometimes wear working clothes or sportswear or 'dress up' for parties or celebrations. In all places of the world, near and far, people wear clothes that suit the way that they live. Clothes are one of the things that make us who we are.

For the reason that follows

Focus

To show the importance of being able to justify an opinion.

You will need

Seven large cards printed with the letters: a, b, c, e, e, s, u; a painting with lots of potential for discussion.

Opening

Choose seven volunteers and give each one a letter card. Ask for another volunteer to unscramble the letters and make the word: **b-e-c-a-u-s-e**. Point out that this word can be split into two smaller words, 'be' and 'cause', and that it means 'for this reason'.

Hold up the painting and ask the children to look at it carefully. Make a quick list of facts about this picture. Explain that you are going to ask them for opinions about the picture but that they will also need to explain why they have decided to have that opinion. Model how you want this done by writing your own opinion on the flip chart under three headings:

Opinion: *I like this picture…*

Why: *because…*

Reason: *…it makes me feel peaceful and calm.*

Now take opinions from the assembly.

Development

Read the poem 'The First Tooth' by Charles and Mary Lamb.

80

Through the house what busy joy,
Just because the infant boy
Has a tiny tooth to show!

I have got a double row,
All as white and all as small;
Yet no one cares for mine at all.

He can say but half a word,
Yet that single sound's preferred
To all the words that I can say
In the longest summer day.

He cannot walk, yet if he put
With mimic motion out his foot,
As if he thought he were advancing,
It's prized more than my best dancing.

Talk about the facts in the poem (the writer can do everything the baby can – he can talk, he can walk, he can even dance). Discuss the children's view of how the writer must be feeling. Ensure that they justify their opinions by referring to the evidence. Ask the children if they have any value judgements to add to these opinions. Is it fair to feel this way? Why not? Ask for a show of hands. Have any children felt similar feelings of being ignored, left out and jealous? Conclude by asking if anyone has a suggestion to help the writer to feel better about the situation.

⌐ *Reflection*

'Because' is an important word. We use it to explain how we are feeling and to give reasons why something happened in the way that it did. 'Because' helps us to give reasons for our behaviour and helps others to understand us. When we are listening to other people it is important that we listen carefully and think about their reasons for feeling the way that they do. Then we can help them to feel better too.

The air that we breathe

Focus

Feeling good through fitness and health.

You will need

Lively dance music; relaxation music; flip-chart; stopwatch.

Opening

Use the following script to guide the children through the assembly.

Who knows some of the things we need if we want to stay healthy?

Make a list of the children's suggestions on the flipchart.

There is something else that our body needs. It goes in our noses and out again every moment of the day and night. Who can guess what I'm talking about? Yes, we need lots and lots of good clean air if we are going to stay healthy.

Ask the children to take a deep breath, hold it, and then let it out slowly. Repeat. Explain that when we breathe in, air goes into our lungs. Our lungs are protected by our ribs. (Get the children to feel their ribs as they breathe in and out.)

⏭ Development

Our lungs are a wonderful part of our body. When we need to use a lot of energy, they start to work harder and they move more quickly. Would some of you like to come up and show everybody how this happens?

Ask for some confident volunteers to come forward. Begin by getting them to count their breaths for 20 seconds. Put on some lively dance music and invite the children to jump or dance around energetically. Now ask them to count their breathing rate again.

The number is higher because your lungs have been working harder to get more air into your bodies. The more regular exercise we do, the stronger our lungs get. That means we can breathe in much more air to help give us more energy for life. Another way that air can help us to stay healthy is when we use it to help ourselves to calm down, rest and relax. When we do this, we breathe deeply and slowly. We can all have a go at that now.

Put on the relaxation music and continue with the following script:

Make sure you are comfortable. Close your eyes and sit very still. Listen to your breathing. Can you feel the air going in and out? Just listen to the sound of your breath for a moment and let your mind become very still.

Take a long slow breath and let it out very gently, like this. Your breathing is slow and calm, your mind is calm. Calm and slow. Calm and relaxed.

Pretend that you are a smooth round pebble on the beach. The sun is shining on you and you feel lovely and warm.

You are a beautiful pebble and you can feel a gentle breeze blowing all around you. You can hear the sea making a shhh, shhh noise not far away down the beach. You love sitting on the beach in the sunshine.

Now it is time for you to turn back into a boy or girl again. Gently shake your shoulders and arms. Wiggle your fingers and toes. Our bodies need air when we are awake and when we are asleep. When we need energy we breath in a lot of air and when we relax we need to breathe deeply and slowly.

Reflection

We keep our teeth healthy by remembering to brush them every day. We can keep our lungs healthy by taking exercise. We need to look after our bodies and keep them healthy and strong for every new day.

Relationships

Empathy and awareness of the needs of others is covered in the following assemblies, particularly in the context of family and close relationships.

'What can I do for you?' considers what it means to be unselfish. In this assembly, a Native American fable tells the story of a coyote who helped out humankind long ago, because he knew people were suffering. This 'thinking of others' focus continues in 'Easy life', encouraging children to look for ways to make life easier for the people who help them in school.

This theme also offers a chance to see how our feelings can affect other people. 'Keeping steady' explores the idea of balancing our emotions and realising that tipping too far in one direction or another can be avoided.

'The frog prince' is a favourite tale that is used here to look at trust. The princess made a promise and nearly didn't keep it. But in the end, she thought about her own behaviour and how she would be making someone else feel.

The effect of our impact on others is continued in 'Watch me use my ears', where the children are invited to consider how the attention they pay to others is important. No one feels appreciated if it appears they are being ignored!

Having thought about ourselves and the ways we can interact in a caring way, the section closes with two assemblies that reaffirm the need to appreciate the people who care for our well-being every day.

What can I do for you?

Focus

To investigate what it means to be unselfish.

You will need

No props are required.

Opening

Make a list of a few words that are built upon the core word of selfish: 'self'. You can choose some from the following list:

-self: myself, yourself, himself, herself
Self-: self-assured, self-centred, self-catering, self-confident, self-conscious, self-contained, self-control, self-defence, self-indulgent, selfish, self-esteem, selfless, self-made, self-pity, self-portrait, self-respect, self-sufficient.

Highlight two opposite words – selfish/unselfish – and ask the children to offer suggestions about the meaning of these two words.

Now read the story 'How Coyote Stole Fire', which is a very old tale from the Pacific Northwest of America.

Long ago men were hungry and unhappy. They were cold. The only fire in the world was on a mountain top, watched by three Skookums. They guarded the fire carefully. Men might steal it and become as strong as Skookums.

Coyote wanted men to be warm and happy. One day he crept to the mountain top and watched the Skookums. He watched all day and all night. They thought he was only a skulking coyote.

Coyote saw that one Skookum always sat by the fire. When one went into the tepee, another came out and sat by the fire. Only when the dawn wind arose

was there a chance to steal fire. Then the Skookum, shivering, hurried into the tepee. She called, 'Sister, sister, get up and watch the fire'. But the sister was slow.

Coyote went down the mountainside and called a great council of the animals. He knew if he stole fire, the Skookums would chase him. Coyote said the other animals must help him.

Again Coyote skulked to the mountain top. The Skookums saw only a coyote shivering in the bushes.

When the dawn wind arose, the Skookum on guard called: 'Sister, sister, get up and watch the fire'. But the sister was slow. Coyote seized the fire and jumped down the mountainside. Quickly Skookum followed him. She caught the tip of his tail in her hand; therefore it is white, even to this day.

But Coyote reached Wolf. Wolf seized the fire and leaped down the mountain. Skookum chased Wolf. But Wolf reached Squirrel. Squirrel seized the fire and leaped from branch to branch down the mountain. The fire was so hot it burned the back of his neck. You can see the black spot there, even to this day. The fire was so hot it made Squirrel's tail curl up over his back. Skookum chased Squirrel.

But Squirrel reached Frog. Frog took the coals of fire in his mouth and hopped away. Skookum chased Frog. She caught his tail in her hand. Frog jumped away but Skookum kept the tail. That is why frogs have no tail, even to this day. Soon Skookum caught up with Frog again. To save fire, Frog spit it out on Wood. Wood swallowed it.

Skookum did not know how to get the fire out of Wood. But Coyote did. Coyote showed Man how to get fire out of wood by rubbing two dry sticks together, as they do even to this day.

Explain any details that may be unfamiliar. Skookums are nasty spirits and, long ago, fire was made by rubbing two sticks together.

▶▶ *Development*

Talk about the behaviour of Coyote, Wolf, Squirrel, Frog and the Skookums.

Who was mean and selfish and who was generous and unselfish?

Did the animals steal fire for themselves?

Who did they steal it for?

Why did they steal it for Man? (Because they bothered to notice that he was cold and hungry.)

Was it easy for them? (No, they had to work hard and some of them were hurt.)

How did Man feel about what the animals did for him?

Ask the children to think about times when people around them are unselfish (picking up their toys, putting up with the noise they sometimes make). Are there situations when they could be unselfish? Take suggestions (for example, to let someone choose a game, be quiet when a carer has a headache, help a friend to learn a new skill, let someone else be the centre of attention sometimes). Ask for volunteers to role-play scenarios to show how people can be unselfish.

💭 *Reflection*

Sometimes we need to stand up for ourselves and make sure that we get the things that we need. But at other times we must think about what other people need. We need to be unselfish and make other people happy because...

Little deeds of kindness,
Little words of love
Help to make earth happy
Like the heaven above.

Julia Carney

An easy life

Focus

Looking at ways to help teachers and support staff in school.

You will need

Two big cards (write the word 'hard' on one and 'easy' on the other); some simple prepared tasks for the children to perform (see below); flip chart and pens.

Opening

Ask for two volunteers. Explain that you have a little job for them to do. Pick up the cards and show all the children that one card says 'easy' and the other says 'hard'. Put the cards behind your back and shuffle them about. Ask one volunteer to choose a card as you say the words:

Will it be easy?

Will it be hard

Pick a hand

And choose a card…

Reveal the card that the volunteer has chosen. The other child gets the remaining card. Each child then tackles a similar task which has been made easy or difficult depending on their card. For example, before the assembly, give two members of staff (Mrs Brown and Mrs Green) a book and tell them to hide it in their bag.

Easy task – ask the child to fetch the book from Mrs Brown.
Hard task – tell the child that someone in the room is holding a book, but you are not going to say who that person is. They will have to ask around.

Devise two or three other tasks to reinforce your point. For example, you could get one child to hop across the floor with a beanbag on their head while the other one walks.

⏭ *Development*

Let's think about the job of the lunchtime supervisor. What things can you do to make lining-up easy or hard for your supervisor?

Make a list under the headings easy/hard. Do the same with other routine school situations. It would be a good idea to do a little research beforehand and ask all members of staff to suggest areas where the children's behaviour might need a little attention.

Think about the tasks that our two volunteers had to perform. Which did they prefer – the hard tasks or the easy tasks? With a little thought, we can give others the 'easy' card every day.

💭 *Reflection*

Each and every one of us has two invisible cards. One says 'easy' and the other says 'hard'. Each and every one of us can choose which card we will use. We should all try our best to make good choices and to help the people who are here to look after us.

Keeping steady

 ## Focus

To investigate strategies that help us to balance our moods.

 ## You will need

A long ruler; a bench with safety mats either side.

 ## Opening

Invite volunteers to come forward and attempt to balance a ruler on their hand, finger, or head. Point out the reasons why the ruler sometimes falls: it moves too much in one direction or another. Ask for more volunteers to walk up and down the bench. (If you prefer, you can draw a line on the floor and pretend that it is a tightrope.) Ask each volunteer to demonstrate balancing and falling by leaning to the left or right and doing other little stunts: turn round, stand on one leg and so on.

Balancing is all about staying steadily on the centre of the straight and narrow line. Too much leaning in either direction causes the gymnast or tightrope walker to falter. This is especially true when he/she is doing something complicated. What does the gymnast do in order to stay steady? (Stop, think, take things slowly.)

▶▶ Development

Life is often like a balancing act. We need to make sure that we don't lean too far into some of our emotions because then we can get the wobbles and lose control of our feelings in just the same way that the gymnast can lose control of their body. If we start wobbling, we need to remember what the gymnast does to regain balance.

Ask the children to contribute strategies that help them to balance themselves when they get over-emotional. Give prompts if necessary:

Stop
Take things slowly
Concentrate
Count to ten
Breathe deeply and steadily

Invite confident volunteers to act out scenarios: getting too excited at a birthday party, being scared at night, losing your temper in the playground. Ask them to show the 'wobble' and then model balancing techniques.

☁ *Reflection*

Each of us feels many different emotions through every single day. Each of us needs to learn how to stay in charge of our emotions and not to let our feelings lead us over the edge. When we are not careful we can allow our emotions to overpower us and that is when accidents and trouble can happen. We need to be like gymnasts and tightrope walkers and make sure that we stay balanced. We do this by making ourselves calm; by stopping and thinking and concentrating on making our breathing steady and regular. Then we are back in charge of our feelings instead of our feelings being in charge of us.

The Frog Prince

 Focus

To investigate what it means to keep a promise.

 What you need

Four containers, each containing an item we would keep (a sweet, a ring, a picture of a kitten, a pen, a birthday card etc) and something we would discard (a bit of crumpled paper, a broken pen top, an empty crisp packet etc).

 Opening

Ask for four volunteers from the audience. Give the first child a container and speak this rhyme.

What will you lose?
What will you keep?
It's your turn to choose,
Take a peek...

The child then shows the audience what she has found and decides which item to keep and which to discard. Ask the child to explain how she will keep the item safe. Reinforce everyone's understanding of the word 'keep' by saying: 'Sam is keeper of the ring and she will keep it safe.' Continue until every container has been opened.

When we keep something we are choosing to look after it and are keeping it safe for the future.

▶▶ *Development*

Explain that sometimes we need to keep things that we can't see or touch.

Who knows what a promise is? When do we make promises and why do we need to keep them? Has anyone heard the phrases 'to give your word' and 'to keep your word'? How do we feel when someone breaks a promise?

Read the story of the Frog Prince (see below). There are many beautifully written versions of this story which you may prefer to use. The following version is brief and is designed to enable you to *ad lib* and lead the children though a series of tableaux.

Long ago, and far away, there lived a beautiful princess who was always happy. Every afternoon she would go out into the garden and play with her favourite golden ball. One day she missed the ball and it bounced away and fell into a deep, dark well. The princess was upset and sat down to cry, but she jumped when an ugly frog sprang out of the well and looked up at her.

'What will you give me if I find your ball?' he asked.

The princess listened, and then she thought, and then she replied that she would give him anything he asked for.

'Do you promise?' asked the frog.

'Oh yes, I promise,' replied the princess.

So the frog jumped into the well and found the beautiful golden ball.

The princess was delighted. She picked up the ball and turned to go back to the palace but the frog called out to her.

'You promised,' he said, 'and I wish to come with you and be your special friend.'

The princess looked at him in amazement and ran back home as fast as she could. The poor frog felt sad and lonely.

The next day, there was a knock at the door and a croaking voice called out, 'Princess, you must keep your promise.'

The princess was afraid. She paced up and down and worried about the promise she had made but had not kept. Then she felt ashamed, so she straightened herself up, opened the door and allowed the frog to come in.

'I will be your friend,' she said.

Then a magical thing happened to the frog. He began to change and grow and turn into a handsome prince with a big smile on his face.

RELATIONSHIPS – The Frog Prince

'Thank you,' he said, 'A wicked witch put a spell on me and turned me into a frog. Only a princess who kept her promise could break the spell.'

And, of course, the princess was proud that she had kept a promise!

Remind the children of the choices that the princess chose to make and the reward she received for keeping her promise. Ask for volunteers to come forward and act or mime the story.

Reflection

If we have a pet we do everything we can to keep it safe and happy. When we own something very expensive, we do the same. Whether it's a new computer or a diamond ring, we look after it and keep it in a safe place so that it doesn't get spoiled or broken. All our promises are special things too. We must always try to keep our promises because a promise freely given is more valuable than gold.

Watch me use my ears

Focus

Developing the skill of attentive listening.

You will need

A colleague; a piece of stirring classical music.

Opening

Remind the children that we have five senses and tell them that they are going to be thinking about two very important senses today: seeing and hearing. Prepare everyone to sit calmly and listen to the music.

We all hear with our ears, and the music we are going to hear will move through the air in invisible waves until it reaches our ears and we hear it as sound.

Development

Thank the children for listening. Pause and try to look a little confused as if you can't quite understand what you have just done. Point at the CD player and look at the children as if you are trying to work something out.

I've just thanked you for listening so well but I told you earlier that sound waves are invisible. So how did I know that you were listening to the music? Can anyone tell me what you did that showed me that you were listening?

Take suggestions from the floor and list them on the flip-chart.

I've noticed something important about the list that shows good listening. They are all things that we can see! We use our eyes to see if someone is listening with their ears.

Ask a colleague to come to the front and help to demonstrate this as you make a couple of short speeches (about anything you like). During the speech, the colleague needs to model an example of either good or poor listening behaviour: leaning towards you and nodding, or staring at the ceiling, yawning and so on. At the end of each demonstration, ask the children to vote on whether your colleague was really listening.

Listening is not just something we can see but is also something that changes how we feel. When we know that someone is actively listening, we feel happy and warm inside but when someone just won't listen, we can feel sad and neglected.

☁ *Reflection*

Remind the children that you have all been thinking about two important senses, hearing and seeing. We decide if someone is really listening to us by noticing what they are doing as they listen.

Feeling 'listened to' is very important. When we feel that we have been heard, we feel happy and cared for but we feel lonely and unwanted when no-one will listen to us properly. Good friends and classmates will always want those around them to feel happy, so we must all remember to show that we are listening to one another.

Play the music again and allow the children to practise their listening skills for a few moments.

Helping Henry

 Focus

To appreciate the people who care for us.

 You will need

A soft toy to play the role of Henry; a bag containing items for Henry's holiday packing: useful (sandwiches, a blanket, a toothbrush, a cuddly toy of his own) and not-so-useful (a jar of floor polish, a piece of string, a piece of wallpaper); large blank cards and a marker pen.

 Opening

Use the following script to guide the children through your introduction:

I'm a bit flustered today because I've got two jobs to do instead of one. I've got my normal job at school but I have another one too. My Auntie Ethel came to visit me yesterday evening and said that she's going to Scotland to visit the Loch Ness monster. Do you know what she did then? She gave me Henry and said that I had to take care of him while she's gone. Would you like to meet him?

Show the children the cuddly toy.

She also gave me this bag of his things. The problem is that my Auntie Ethel is very disorganised. She has stuffed all sorts of things into the bag and I need some help to get it sorted out. Do you think that you could help me?

Choose one volunteer at a time, and ask each one to put a hand into the bag and pull out an item. As you go along, ask the children to sort them into two groups: things that Henry needs (eg sandwiches, a blanket, a toothbrush, cuddly toy) and things that Henry doesn't need (eg jar of floor polish, piece of string, piece of wallpaper). Now look together at the two piles of objects.

Henry seems to need rather a lot of things. Does he get them by himself? No, he needs Auntie Ethel (and all of you children) to look after him. He needs people to take care of him.

▶ Development

We all need people to take care of our needs. Our carers keep us safe and healthy every hour of the day and night, every day of the week. They take responsibility for our well-being. They make breakfast for us in the morning and they check that the front door is locked safely last thing at night. Can you tell me one thing that your mum and dad and carers do for you?

Take suggestions from the floor. As each child comes forward with their suggestion, help them to form groups (for example, all those who mention breakfast, lunch etc can stand together grouped as food). Keep going until you have sizeable groups. Recap all the different things that parents/carers do to help us, and then sort the children again into categories such as safe, happy and healthy. Write the words on to cards and ask a child from each group to hold them up.

☁ Reflection

The people who care for us look after our needs. They care for us in so many different ways. They make sure that we are safe and they make sure that we are healthy. They look after us when we are ill and they cuddle us when we are unhappy. Even when they are tired, they still make sure that we are well cared for. So let's all go home tonight and give our carers a big hug and say 'thank you very much' for looking after us so well.

Twinkle

 Focus

The importance of caring for each other.

 You will need

A cuddly toy cat; a tin of cat food and any other items relevant to caring for a cat; a flip-chart and pens.

 Opening

Hold up the toy cat and tell the children that you have brought in a special pet – Twinkle the cat. Give the children a few details about his habits and show them the items that a pet needs to stay healthy and happy.

A great many people are needed to produce the things that Twinkle likes. Just think about the number of people who are needed to make this tin of cat food. Think of all the people who work to make the contents, make the tin, transport it to the shop, put it on the self and sell it to the pet owner. But Twinkle has a great many other people who take care of her. Can you tell me who any of those people are? What sort of things do they do?

Take suggestions from the assembly (such as combing, feeding, cleaning, taking to the vet and so on).

So, it sounds like Twinkle has everyone she needs to make her healthy, safe and happy. She is a very lucky cat, isn't she!

▶▶ Development

Let's think about all of you now. Can you think of all the people who come into school every day to make sure that you are healthy, safe and happy?

Take suggestions from the children and write the names on the flipchart (don't

100

forget people such as the postman and milkman). When suggestions run out, count up to see how many people you have listed.

We have thought of lots of people who look after us at school. I think that we should thank them all for keeping us healthy, safe and happy.

Write 'Thank you very much' at the bottom of the list.

There are a lot of other people who help one another at school. Can you guess who they are? YOU, of course. I know that all of you help each other, and the staff, in many different ways. Let's make today a 'thank you day' to remind ourselves of how much we all need each other. Let's make sure that we thank all of the people who help us today.

Reflection

At home, at school and everywhere we go, we live with other people. We are all part of a community. We all need to help one another and make sure that each one of us is safe, healthy and happy. Everyone here can help to make that happen. Let's make every day a helpful day and look after one another. Let every day be a 'thank you day'.

Changes

Two different processes of change are considered in this theme. 'Time for a change' raises issues of motivation and looks at how we can decide to make things happen. It uses Lent to illustrate how sometimes we need willpower to make positive changes.

In 'Butterfly school' there is the perfect opportunity to close the school year with a look at change that happens naturally, and all the wonderful things that can happen while we are too busy to notice. Use this final assembly to celebrate achievement in your school and to help everyone realise just how far they have travelled in a short space of time.

Time for a change

Focus

Investigating the process of change.

You will need

A small duvet and two covers; a camp-bed (or row of chairs to serve as a bed); peaceful instrumental music.

Opening

Show the children the duvet with its cover on. Invite five volunteers to queue up and, one at a time, get under the duvet, snuggle up, wake and get up. Keep the pace very fast like a speeded-up film.

The duvet cover has taken quite a battering from all those people getting in and out, hasn't it? Now it's looking a bit crumpled and grubby. Do you know what we need to do? Yes, we need to change it!

Ask for two volunteers to change the cover. Choose small children who will find the task difficult. Talk the children through this process of change.

First we have to remove the old cover. The duvet looks stripped and bare and a bit lonely without its bright cover. Putting on a new duvet cover requires thought and effort, doesn't it?

Make a bit of a drama of this stage: let the volunteers get into a muddle and fumble before they get it right. Point out how good the duvet looks and feels now that you have made the effort to change it.

⏭ Development

Just as you made the decision to change the duvet cover, people need to take a look at themselves from time to time and decide if they need to make some changes. Change can feel uncomfortable at first because we feel as if we have lost something familiar, just as the duvet lost its old cover and looked bare. We have to concentrate and make the effort to fit the changes into our lives. (You could give examples like giving up chips and learning to like salad!)

All over the world and throughout history, people have come together to do just this. For Christians, this time is called Lent. During Lent they remember the time when Jesus went into the desert and fasted for 40 days and work together to change into better people. Before Lent can begin, Christians have a day when they 'strip the cupboards bare'. We call this day Shrove Tuesday but the French call it Mardi Gras or 'Fat Tuesday'. They use up all the eggs and butter and cream in readiness for the time when they will eat plain food and remember Jesus' suffering. Nowadays we use these ingredients to make pancakes.

It is also a time for people to think about other things that they can do to live less selfish lives. They think about making sacrifices so that other people's lives can be improved. They think about how they can change their behaviour and make themselves better people.

Give some examples such as deciding to stop daydreaming in the classroom and concentrate on listening and learning instead. Ask for volunteers to tell the assembly about the kind of changes people may choose to make. What changes could everyone, as a school, make for Lent? An example might be deciding to show more gratitude to lunchtime staff by queuing quietly in the canteen. List the suggestions on your flip chart and agree to follow through on some of them. Remind the children that you know that changing can seem difficult at first but that it is well worth the effort.

☁ *Reflection*

A pope from the Catholic Church once said some words about Lent that are useful to us all. He used the word penance to describe what we do when we feel the need to change and improve our way of living.

Ask the children to sit quietly with their eyes closed and read the pope's words. Simplify the text as appropriate.

Penance is not just an effort, a weight, but it is also a joy. Sometimes it is a great joy of the human spirit, and a delight that other sources cannot bring forth. Lent is a call to this joy that comes from the effort of patiently finding oneself again. Let no one be afraid to make this effort.

Play some quiet music and give the children a little time to think about changes they could make that require some effort.

Butterfly school

 Focus

Celebrating children's achievements over the year.

 You will need

Images showing the life stages of a butterfly; contributions from other staff members or their classes.

 Opening

Use the following script to guide the children through the assembly.

It is nearly the end of another year. A year can seem like a long time, especially at your age. Who knows how many months have gone by since the last time we had a December? Does anyone know how many days that is? (You may need to provide the answer to this one!) That's a very long time isn't it? A lot can happen in a year full of days. Let's look at how an egg turns into a caterpillar and then a butterfly over time.

Show the images of the butterfly's life stages, and use this script:

At the moment, it is a tiny egg hidden away somewhere safe and it will stay like that for all of the winter. As soon as the weather gets warmer in the spring, it will hatch out of its egg and turn into a caterpillar. That caterpillar will eat and wriggle until the summer ends and then it will turn into a chrysalis and spend next winter doing something wonderful. Do you know what it will be doing? Yes, it will be turning into a butterfly! That's a lot of amazing changes to make in a short space of time.

 Development

Some of you may not have noticed, but you have been making some wonderful changes too. Your teachers and all the other members of staff have been

watching and they have seen you growing up and changing. They say that it's even better than watching a butterfly changing when they notice what some of you have managed to achieve this past year. Everybody in this school has made progress and everyone has grown up quite a bit. Do you realise that you are all much taller?

Line up some children from each year group to show just how much they will have grown.

Do you know that you can do things now that seemed impossible last year? Has anyone learned anything they would like to show us?

Invite volunteers out to the front. Continue by asking other classes to demonstrate their learning and skills. As each class contributes something to this 'variety show' you need to repeat that these are remarkable milestones and that all the children should feel proud of the progress that they have made. You can also use this opportunity to congratulate particular children for hurdles overcome or acts of exceptional conduct. But it is important that the 'everyday' triumphs of everyone are celebrated and rewarded.

⸂ *Reflection*

A year is a very long time. A butterfly changes from an egg into a fully grown butterfly in little more than a year. I think that we have a school full of little butterflies here today. Some of you have changed so fast and the progress you have all made is amazing. You all know and can do so much more than you could a year ago. Well done everyone!

**Why not try our range of 120 quick stand alone
activities and ideas to liven up or
calm down children**

Quality Circle Time has been developed by Jenny Mosley over the past 24 years as
a whole-school approach to enhancing self-esteem, developing positive behaviour
and relationships within the school community. For more information visit our
website www.circle-time.co.uk

ALSO AVAILABLE:
Step-by-Step Guide to Circle Time for SEAL
by Jenny Mosley

This is a first-stop introduction to Quality Circle Time for
beginners and those who want to improve their practice.

For information about training and courses please contact:
Jenny Mosley Consultancies
28A Gloucester Road
Trowbridge BA14 0AA
Tel: 01225 767157
Fax: 01225 755631
Email: circletime@jennymosley.co.uk

For a catalogue of other books published by Positive Press please contact:
Positive Press
28A Gloucester Road
Trowbridge BA14 0AA
Tel: 01225 719204
Fax: 01225 712187
Email: positivepress@jennymosley.co.uk
Website: www.circle-time.co.uk

*Active Assemblies was so popular that we were
asked to write a sequel*

More Active Assemblies